TEACHING
With the
TOOLS KIDS
REALLY USE

TEACHING
With the
TOOLS KIDS
REALLY USE

Learning With Web and
Mobile Technologies

SUSAN BROOKS-YOUNG

CORWIN
A SAGE Company

For information:

Corwin
A SAGE Company
2455 Teller Road
Thousand Oaks, California 91320
(800) 233-9936
Fax: (800) 417-2466
www.corwin.com

SAGE Ltd.
1 Oliver's Yard
55 City Road
London EC1Y 1SP
United Kingdom

SAGE India Pvt. Ltd.
B 1/I 1 Mohan Cooperative
   Industrial Area
Mathura Road, New Delhi 110 044
India

SAGE Asia-Pacific Pte. Ltd.
33 Pekin Street #02-01
Far East Square
Singapore 048763

Printed in the United States of America

Library of Congress Cataloging-in-Publication Data

Brooks-Young, Susan.
Teaching with the tools kids really use: learning with web and mobile technologies/Susan Brooks-Young.
      p. cm.
Includes bibliographical references and index.
ISBN 978-1-4129-7275-8 (pbk.: alk. paper)
   1. Teachers—Training of—United States.   2. Technological literacy—Standards—United States. 3. Educational technology—Standards—United States.   4. Computer technology—United States. 5. Web 2.0—United States. I. Title.

LB1715.B742 2010
372.3'4—dc22   2009043856

This book is printed on acid-free paper.

10   11   12   13   14   10   9   8   7   6   5   4   3   2   1

Acquisitions Editor:	Arnis Burvikovs
Editorial Assistant:	Joanna Coelho
Production Editor:	Libby Larson
Copy Editor:	Codi Bowman
Typesetter:	C&M Digitals (P) Ltd.
Proofreader:	Theresa Kay
Indexer:	Terri Corry
Cover and Graphic Designer:	Scott Van Atta

Contents

Acknowledgments

Corwin gratefully acknowledges the contributions of the following individuals:

April DeGennaro
Gifted Teacher
Fayette County Board of Education
Fayetteville, GA

Katharine Ferrell
Instructional Coach
Excelsior Springs Middle School
Excelsior Springs, MO

Carol S. Holzberg, PhD
Director of Technology
Greenfield Public Schools
Greenfield, MA

Charity L. B. Jennings
Full-Time Faculty, Education
University of Phoenix
Mesa, AZ

Salika A. Lawrence, PhD
Assistant Professor
William Paterson University of New Jersey
Wayne, NJ

Amy S. C. Leh
Professor
California State University, San Bernardino
San Bernardino, CA

Alexis Ludewig
Third Grade Teacher, Northland Pines School District
General Studies Teacher, Fox Valley Technical College
Appleton, WI

Joseph Staub
Resource Specialist Teacher
Thomas Starr King Middle School
Los Angeles, CA

Michelle Strom
Education Instructor, University of Phoenix
National Board Certified Teacher, Grade 5,
    Seoul American Elementary School
Seoul, ROK

Dr. Karen L. Tichy
Associate Superintendent for Instruction and Special Education
Archdiocese of Saint Louis, Catholic Education Office
Saint Louis, MO

About the Author

Prior to embarking on a career as an author and consultant, **Susan Brooks-Young** spent more than 23 years as a prekindergarten through Grade 8 teacher, site administrator, and technology specialist at a county office of education. Since 1986, she has written articles, columns, and reviews for a variety of education journals. She has published a number of books about technology for education leaders, which have received international attention. Susan focuses much of her energy on working with school leaders on their role in successfully implementing instructional technology programs. To that end, she works on a variety of international projects. Susan is also a regular speaker at national and international conferences.

When not on the road, Susan and her husband divide their time between their farm on Lopez Island, Washington, and Vancouver, British Columbia, Canada.

Introduction

There was a time, not all that long ago, when industrialized nations may not have ruled the world, but they were certainly on top of it. Good wages, a strong middle class, and security were taken for granted in these countries. But today, the outlook is different. The clothing we wear is manufactured in Thailand or Vietnam. The produce we eat is grown in Mexico or South America. The computers we use are assembled in China.

Offshoring and outsourcing may have been easier to ignore when the greatest impact was on blue-collar workers, but then white-collar jobs began shifting as well. Accountants in India began preparing tax forms online. Radiologists in Asia read X-rays taken in North America. High-tech jobs blossomed in Ireland. Suddenly, the middle class started taking notice. And then, the bottom fell out of financial markets worldwide. Now even the very wealthy are paying attention to how globalization at all levels is affecting them.

In the long run, this flattening of the world can be advantageous for everyone. But to realize these benefits, people from all walks of life, including (and perhaps especially) educators, need to let go of doing business as usual and begin adapting to the changing world. Emerging nations have been quick to pick up the gauntlet—perhaps because they had little to lose and everything to gain. Developed nations have been more resistant to making the changes needed to thrive in this new global society—perhaps because they fear they have everything to lose. But not taking action is a recipe for failure for these nations.

Students who live in industrialized nations around the world are increasingly disenchanted with the education programs being provided. They view educators who use traditional teaching methods as being out of touch. They rankle at completing the same projects and assignments their parents and even grandparents did when they attended school. They believe that the technology tools that are banned on campus are, in fact, the keys to success in their future.

The purpose of this book is to encourage school administrators, teachers, and support staff to look at mobile technologies and Web 2.0 tools that students use on a regular basis away from school but that have not yet made their way into mainstream education. These inexpensive and sometimes even free technologies and tools could be used to revolutionize teaching and learning, but they have yet to gain widespread acceptance in educational circles.

The topics covered in the book fall roughly into three sections, book-ended by Chapter 1, which introduces 21st-century skills, and Chapter 10, which discusses issues surrounding digital citizenship. Chapters 2 through 4 examine inexpensive hardware in the form of mobile technologies that most students own or have access to, such as cell phones, netbooks, and MP3 players. These technologies could, with very little effort, make it possible to implement one-to-one computing initiatives in every school—if they were permitted on campus. Chapters 5 through 9 each take a look at Web 2.0 tools such as blogs, wikis, and social networks that can be used to support collaboration and communication in virtually any instructional environment—if they weren't blocked by network filters. Each chapter provides basic information about the emerging technology or tool being discussed along with strategies and practical suggestions for classroom use.

Discussion questions are also included in each of the first 10 chapters. These can be used to lead group talks in faculty and staff meetings, to provide guidance in planning committees or in a variety of adult learning situations. And each chapter includes extensive bibliographic references for further reading. Every effort has been made to provide up-to-date Web addresses (URLs) for these references. However, because of the changing face of the Internet, it is not possible to avoid updates that may result in new URLs. In this case, it is nearly always possible to find the site or article by searching using the title as the keyword(s).

What these chapters do not include is many references to research about whether the use of technology impacts student performance. This is not an oversight. Although many detractors appear to be stuck on this issue, it's asking the wrong question. For one thing, little research has been done because use in schools has been limited. But more important, most employers, parents, and students believe that the purpose of the prekindergarten through Grade12 education system is to prepare pupils to be successful in the existing workplace and in their personal lives. If this belief is true, our charge is to identify and use the tools that will best prepare students to function in society now and in the near future.

In other words, it is incumbent upon educators to create engaging learning environments that mirror the real world and to ensure that students acquire the skills needed to function in these settings. Today, that means learning how to use various technology-based tools effectively and ethically, but this will change again. To remain relevant, these learning environments will continually need to evolve as new technologies take root in the workplace. So what we need to ask is whether our schools are serving students well by providing up-to-date, relevant tools for learning the skills they need to lead successful lives.

These chapters also do not include references to multiple model projects. This is because projects where students are permitted to use the mobile technologies and Web 2.0 tools favored by students are few and far between and, in most cases, are very recent innovations. Where possible, good examples of models are mentioned; however, it is important to remember that, at this time, we find ourselves in the equivalent of the frontier. Until we are able to openly explore effective uses of these technologies as tools for teaching and learning, we are not going to be able to cite good models.

The final chapter of the book focuses on practical strategies for identifying and implementing use of emerging mobile technologies and Web 2.0 tools for instruction. This chapter includes a discussion about current issues and provides a decision-making model that can be used when selecting emerging mobile technologies and Web 2.0 tools for classroom use. The model includes tables to complete during information gathering and questions for discussion prior to making decisions. Because this field is rapidly changing, the tables provided in the model are open-ended to ensure applicability for some time to come.

Effective education is the foundation of successful societies. But in recent years, at least in developed countries, the survival of the existing institution seems to have trumped the importance of providing relevant, timely instruction. This trend can be changed, but the time to take action is now. One way to move education forward is to embrace emerging technologies that make it possible to implement programs where students master core academic content, hone applied 21st-century skills, and learn how to find success in an increasingly digital world.

21st-Century Skills 1

Education may be the most successful institution to emerge from the Industrial Age. First-world nations have thrived because they identified and employed effective strategies for educating the general population so citizens were well prepared to succeed in the 20th-century workforce and society. This strength may now become the downfall of education in these countries.

The world is changing. Rapid advances in technology have changed the way services are provided and goods are manufactured. It's difficult, if not impossible, to find an industry that has not changed because of these advances, and many people now have access to myriad goods and services that didn't exist a decade ago. Experts predict that advances will continue to accelerate for at least the next 10 to 15 years. This growth will continue to spur change in the worldwide workforce as economic globalization continues to spread.

The critical question facing educators in all first-world nations today is, What are we doing to prepare our students for this new world? To date, the answer is not much. In his book, *The World Is Flat: A Brief History of the Twenty-First Century*, Thomas Friedman (2006) writes that his advice to his daughters is as follows:

> Girls, when I was growing up, my parents used to say to me, "Tom, finish your dinner—people in China and India are starving." My advice to you is: "Girls, finish your homework—people in China and India are starving for your jobs." And in a flat world, they can have them, because in a flat world there is no such thing as an American job. There is just a job, and in more cases than ever before it will go to the best, smartest, most productive, or cheapest worker—wherever he or she resides. (p. 277)

Being confident that educators can prepare students for this new world is based on the assumption that they have some idea of what to prepare them *for.* And actually, they do. Education and business leaders

21st-Century Skills: The content knowledge and applied skills that today's students need to master to thrive in a continually evolving workplace and society.

have spent the last decade grappling with what students need to know and be able to do to find success in the 21st century. This skill set is often referred to as **21st-century skills.**

WHAT ARE 21ST-CENTURY SKILLS?

Twenty-first-century skills comprise both content knowledge and applied skills that today's students need to master to thrive in a continually evolving workplace and society. Educators typically refer to three documents when discussing 21st-century skills. The first document, *enGauge 21st Century Skills for 21st Century Students*, was published in partnership by the North Central Regional Educational Laboratory (NCREL) and the Metiri Group (2003a). Couched in academic achievement, this document identifies four broad areas of applied skills where today's students must also excel: (1) digital age literacy, (2) inventive thinking, (3) effective communication, and (4) high productivity. Each broad area is further defined by subtopics designed to identify specific skills. A second document, *enGauge 21st Century Skills: Literacy in the Digital Age* (2003b), further explains this skills framework.

The second document frequently referenced in relationship to 21st-century skills is the refreshed National Educational Technology Standards for Students (NETS*S), which were released by the International Society for Technology in Education (ISTE) in June 2007. Although technology-support instruction is the overriding focus of this updated set of standards, applied 21st-century skills are woven throughout the six standards and performance indicators, as is evident in the titles of the six standards areas: (1) creativity and innovation; (2) communication and collaboration; (3) research and information fluency; (4) critical thinking, problem solving, and decision making; (5) digital citizenship; and (6) technology operations and concepts.

The final document is the *Framework for 21st Century Skills*, published by the Partnership for 21st Century Skills and updated in January 2009. This framework stresses the importance of basing instruction of applied skills in the context of core academic subjects and identifies four areas: (1) core subjects and 21st-century themes; (2) learning and innovation skills; (3) information, media, and technology skills; and (4) life and career skills. As is the case with the enGauge framework, subtopics are identified in each of the four main areas, and the Partnership for 21st Century Skills Web site offers a variety of supporting documents.

As you can see, common themes are found in all three documents. As educators work to align curricula to these standards, it's important to remember that they do not replace content area standards; they support them by emphasizing the importance of using modern tools and strategies to achieve academic goals. Practical suggestions provided in each chapter in this book reflect this approach by identifying ways the hardware or Web-based tool can be used to support content area instruction.

COMMON OBJECTIONS TO
TEACHING 21ST-CENTURY SKILLS

The worldwide trend toward increased accountability in education outcomes is, at face value, a good thing. Some educators fear that in practice this drive for accountability all too often ends up narrowing focus to achievement of basic proficiency. Time, energy, and resources are devoted to bringing student performance up to minimal standards in math, reading, and writing with other disciplines getting short shrift. On the other hand, in their editorial opinion piece, "Before 21st Century Skills, Teach Basics," which appeared in the *Boston Globe* on November 29, 2008, Charles Chieppo and Jim Stergios argue that teaching 21st-century skills is tantamount to requiring "a shift from an unwavering focus on enduring academic content and raising student achievement to one that favors jargon and the politically connected" (¶ 13).

Recently, Eric Donald Hirsch Jr., founder of the Core Knowledge Foundation, and Ken Kay, cofounder of the Partnership for 21st Century Skills, were interviewed for an article published in *USA Today*, "What to Learn, 'Core Knowledge' or '21st Century Skills'?" (Toppo, 2009). Hirsch argues that the key to a good education is specific, year-by-year curricula. Kay counters that it's not an either/or proposition, stating that today's students need to pursue both content and skills. The sticking point seems to be how to do both well.

In reality, this is not a new debate, at least in U.S. education circles. In the late 19th century, educators were arguing whether the driving purpose of high school should be to prepare students for college or if the curriculum should be revised to serve all students. The National Education Association established the Committee of Ten in 1892 to explore national standardization of the secondary curriculum. The committee worked for two years and published a report in 1894 in which a number of recommendations were made that still influence education in the United States today. Perhaps one of the most important findings was that secondary education should help all students flourish, whether they were college bound or not (Center for the Study of Mathematics Curriculum, 1994).

It may be that what we really need to grapple with is the fact that our current system of education no longer helps all students flourish. There are a variety of reasons this statement is true, ranging from the fact that we are educating a different population from what we dealt with in the past to the fact that our digital-age workplace places very different demands on our graduates. But the bottom line is that approximately 30% of our high school–aged students do not graduate in four years. The impact of dropping out of school is both individual and societal. Lifetime earnings for students who do not graduate are just 60% of someone who has a high school diploma, and dropouts are more likely to require more resources from social programs or end up in the prison system than are high school graduates (Fields, 2008).

CHANGING VIEWPOINTS

The first decade of the 21st century is now behind us and little has changed in public education in the United States. However, public opinion about the importance of teaching 21st-century skills in school is shifting. Public Opinion Strategies and Peter D. Hart Research Associates conducted a national survey of registered voters in September 2007 (Partnership for 21st Century Skills, n.d.). The purpose of the survey was to capture public opinion about teaching 21st-century skills in American schools. The survey results showed that although respondents did not want schools to back away from teaching basic content skills such as reading, writing, and math, they also want schools to teach skills in technology use, critical thinking, ethics and social responsibility, and other 21st-century skills. In fact, 99% of respondents said they believe that teaching these skills is critical for future economic success in the United States (Partnership for 21st Century Skills, n.d.).

The Speak Up Project conducts an annual survey of students, parents, teachers, and administrators across the United States to track stakeholders' opinions about key 21st-century issues as they relate to education. The 2007 findings, reported in April 2008, also reveal some shifts in attitudes. For example, for the first time since the survey's inception in 2003, 60% of parents and 73% of teachers rate good technology skills as being important in the 21st century, and teachers and school leaders identified one-to-one computing as a key component for 21st-century classrooms. In addition, although students put a higher value on teamwork and developing creativity than the adult participants, both parents and teachers rank good communication skills as being important for students' future success (Project Tomorrow, 2008).

The push to make significant changes in the skills students are being taught in school is gaining momentum. At least 10 states have formally committed to incorporating 21st-century skills into instruction (Toppo, 2009). Of course, one of the problems is that we do not know precisely what kinds of job skills today's kindergarten students will need when they graduate from high school or college. And it's highly likely that these students will have multiple careers during their work lives. This is why the Partnership for 21st Century Skills (2009) and other like-minded organizations are pressing for curricula that blend more traditional content knowledge with applied skills that we can predict with confidence will be useful, such as information literacy, critical thinking, problem solving, and the like. As Walter Gretzky told his son, ice hockey great, Wayne, "Skate to where the puck is going to be, not to where it has been" (Dryden, 2000, pp. 19–20).

STRATEGIES FOR CLASSROOM USE

It may be time for a revamping of the education system on the scale of what was done by the Committee of Ten. Our current education system is deeply rooted in the Agrarian and Industrial Ages, reflecting the educational needs of first-world nations in the 19th and 20th centuries, but is no longer an appropriate model for today. In a keynote she presented at the Technology Information Center for Administrative Leadership (TICAL) Conference in Little Rock, Arkansas, in February of 2006, Susan Patrick, President and Chief Executive Officer of the International Association for K–12 Online Learning (iNACOL), pointed out that we have actually pushed the system as currently designed beyond its limits. She stated that the existing model was designed for 25% of high school graduates to go on to college, and we currently have a college graduation rate of slightly more than 27%.

What are some of the constraints we face today? To begin with, our annual and daily schedules are problematic. The 180-day (give or take a few days) school year was based on the needs of an agrarian society when students had to work in the fields between May and August. And the daily schedule reflects starting and ending times based on the need for these same students to be back at the farm doing their daily chores.

The curricula taught today present another set of issues. Over the last century, we have made additions to required content but have been loathe to remove anything. As a result, teachers and students face daunting (and most agree impossible) numbers of standards and performance indicators that are supposed to be covered each year. And thanks to lengthy summer breaks, valuable instructional time is lost every fall getting students back up to speed, with additional time lost to mandated testing.

Change on the scale required to make a difference is not under the control of individual teachers or site administrators. But it is still possible for these educators to consider ways that the applied skills found in the *Framework for 21st Century Skills* can be taught in the context of content-based activities. In addition, educators can explore meaningful ways to extend the school day through use of a variety of readily available technologies.

PRACTICAL SUGGESTIONS

When making the decision to embed applied 21st-century skills into content lessons, the importance of preplanning and teamwork cannot be too heavily emphasized. If possible, enlist the cooperation of one or more likeminded colleagues. Begin by reviewing pertinent documents including the *Framework for 21st Century Skills* (Partnership for 21st Century Skills, 2009) and the NETS*S. The number of colleagues working with you will help you determine the number of instructional units you can revise to incorporate applied 21st-century skills.

Visit both the ISTE and Partnership for 21st Century Skills Web sites to find supporting documentation that you can use in planning. For example, the Partnership for 21st Skills site provides links to Milestones for Improving Learning and Education (MILE) Guide for 21st Century Skills, which you can use to assess your current implementation of 21st-century skills and plan for next steps. This site also offers an online tool called Route 21, which provides an overview of the framework and discusses assessment strategies. The ISTE site provides links to the standards and performance indicators as well as to a list of essential conditions for implementing the standards, grade cluster profiles indicating expected skill levels for grade level clusters (prekindergarten through Grade 2, Grades 3 through 5, Grades 6 through 8, and Grades 9 through 12), and other implementation resources.

Review the academic curricula to identify instructional units you will revise. Consider activities that lend themselves well to project-based learning or where students can be encouraged to solve real-world problems. It might be helpful to talk with students to get their ideas about ways lessons could be revised to be both more engaging and to incorporate skills such as critical thinking, communication and collaboration, or information literacy. Students today have very definite views about what constitutes effective use of technology or best strategies for finding and evaluating information. And although students need adult guidance in learning, we can learn more about what engages them and the tools they would like to use in the learning process.

One mistake that teachers often make when updating lesson plans to incorporate 21st-century skills is to simply automate traditional activities. As a result, students are asked to use a word processor to type a paper once it's been handwritten, conduct online research as well as visit the library, or create a five-slide PowerPoint presentation in lieu of creating a science fair poster. Changes at this level do not challenge students to dig more deeply into the content and have little or no impact on overall student performance. The technologies and tools described in subsequent chapters of this book along with practical suggestions for classroom use can be used to transform classroom practice and extend the school day in ways that will have a positive impact on student achievement.

Talk with colleagues and students, review the materials suggested here, and use the suggestions provided in this book to make the changes in your sphere of control that will effectively incorporate 21st-century skills into your teaching.

DISCUSSION POINTS

1. In your judgment, which of the 21st-century skills are most important to teach? Make a prioritized list and explain your top and lowest priorities.

2. Estimate the number of opportunities your students currently have to use 21st-century applied skills during a school year. Is this sufficient? Explain your answer.

3. Imagine you had the authority to transform your school into a 21st-century place of learning. Describe a typical day once changes are implemented.

4. Choose one classroom activity. Revise this activity so it includes applied 21st-century skills.

REFERENCES

Books

Dryden, S. (Ed). (2000). *Total Gretzky: The magic, the legend, the numbers.* Toronto, Ontario, Canada: McClelland & Stewart.

Friedman, T. (2006). *The world is flat: A brief history of the twenty-first century* (Updated and expanded edition). New York: Farrar, Straus, and Giroux.

Web Sites

Core Knowledge Foundation. (2009). http://coreknowledge.org/CK/index.htm.

International Society for Technology in Education (ISTE). (2009). http://www .iste.org/.

Partnership for 21st Century Skills. (2009). Retrieved from http://www.21st centuryskills.org/.

Online Reports and Articles

Center for the Study of Mathematics Curriculum. (2004). *The committee of ten.* Retrieved from http://www.mathcurriculumcenter.org/PDFS/CCM/summaries/ comm_of_10_summary.pdf>.

Chieppo, C., & Stergios, J. (2008, November 29). Before 21st century skills, teach basics. *The Boston Globe.* Retrieved from http://www.boston.com/boston globe/editorial_opinion/oped/articles/2008/11/29/before_21st_century_ skills_teach_basics/

Fields, G. (2008, October 21). The high school dropout's economic ripple effect. *The Wall Street Journal.* Retrieved from http://online.wsj.com/article/ SB122455013168452477.html.

International Society for Technology in Education (ISTE). (2007). *NETS for students.* Retrieved from http://www.iste.org/Content/NavigationMenu/NETS/ ForStudents/NETS_for_Students.htm.

North Central Regional Educational Laboratory (NCREL) and Metiri Group. (2003a). *enGauge 21st century skills for 21st century students.* Retrieved from http://www.bcps.org/offices/lis/staging/activesci/images/litskillsbrochure.pdf.

North Central Regional Educational Laboratory (NCREL) and Metiri Group. (2003b). *enGauge 21st century skills: Literacy in the digital age.* Retrieved from http://www.grrec.ky.gov/SLC_grant/engauge21st_Century_Skills.pdf.

Partnership for 21st Century Skills. (2009, January 2). *Framework for 21st century skills.* Retrieved from http://www.21stcenturyskills.org/index.php? Itemid=120&id=254&option=com_content&task=view.

Project Tomorrow. (2008, April 8). *Speak up 2007 for students, teachers, parents, & school leaders—Selected national findings.* Retrieved from http://www.tomorrow .org/docs/National%20Findings%20Speak%20Up%202007.pdf.

Toppo, G. (2009, March 5). What to learn: "Core knowledge" or "21st century skills"? *USA Today.* Retrieved from http://www.usatoday.com/news/education/ 2009–03–04-core-knowledge_N.htm.

PART I

Mobile Technologies

Setting the Stage for
Chapters 2 Through 4

One-to-one computing is of great interest to many educators, but the costs are usually prohibitive. Students are also keenly aware of having to "power down" before entering most typical school facilities. Chapters 2 through 4 examine inexpensive hardware in the form of mobile technologies that most students own or have access to, such as cell phones, MP3 players, and netbooks. These technologies could, with very little effort, make it possible to implement one-to-one computing initiatives in every school—if they were permitted on campus. However, at this point, few schools encourage or promote wide-scale use of cell phones, MP3 players, or netbooks. The intention of these chapters is to open discussion and exploration of use of these devices as tools for teaching and learning.

Cell Phones   2

Cell phones may be the 21st-century equivalent of chewing gum—at least in education circles. What does this mean? Twentieth-century educators devoted a great deal of time and energy to identifying and disciplining students who chewed gum on campus, with little or no success in actually curtailing its use. Today, many educators appear willing to do the same with cell phones. For example, there are schools where teachers use instructional time at the start and end of each period to collect and then return student cell phones, not understanding that this strategy is often a waste of time.

How does this practice waste time? Because many students are turning over either old, disconnected phones or replica phones, which they have purchased online for about two dollars. Students cheerfully relinquish and retrieve these devices each period while retaining possession of their real phones. If a teacher happens to catch on, the student's loss is minimal. It is far better to find positive ways cell phones can be used as tools for teaching and learning by identifying and enforcing realistic parameters within which students may have cell phones in their possession than to fight what is ultimately a losing—and unnecessary—battle.

But before delving into ways cell phones might be used to support instruction, it's important to understand the rapid and nearly ubiquitous adoption of this technology.

THE SCOOP ON CELL PHONES

Articles about the history of mobile phones frequently reach back to technological developments in the 19th century to begin a discussion of modern mobile communications, but the Federal Communications Commission (FCC) Web site reminds readers that the first *public* cell phone test was not launched until 1977. This program took place in Chicago and involved 2,000 users (FCC, 2004). A little more than 30 years after this initial pilot, the Cellular Telecommunications Industry Association (2008a) estimates that there are 262.7 million cell phone subscribers in the United States alone, representing approximately 84% of all households. Teens make up a large proportion of cell phone subscribers—approximately 79% (about 17 million) of all teens have a cell phone. This is an increase of 36% since 2005 (2008b).

Conventional wisdom usually concludes that cell phone ownership at this level is problematic—symptomatic of a society where families spend little time together and teens isolate themselves. But reports such as "Networked Families" released by the Pew Internet & American Life Project (Kennedy, Smith, Wells, & Wellman, 2008) conclude this simply isn't the case. In fact, the authors of this report found that families are using cell phones and the Internet to compensate for the faster pace of modern life, maintaining closer ties than expected through texting, instant messaging, and other forms of communication. In addition, families who participated in the study reported that although communication has increased when family members are apart, use of communication technology has not decreased face-to-face time.

Although cell phone ownership in general is on the rise, increases in **smart phone** purchases are especially noteworthy. Marketing research firm Strategy Analytics, Inc. predicts that smart phone sales will hit 70.3 million in 2012, up from 18.3 million in 2007 (Kharif, 2008). Currently, 20% of teens who have cell phones are using smart phones, but marketers are betting that this is just the beginning (Olsen, 2008). This is significant because smart phones include features far beyond those of a regular cell phone, including PC-like capabilities. This leads some manufacturers to hope that smart phones might even replace laptops in classrooms (Kharif). In addition, cell phone ownership among students ages 18 and under is not limited to teens. Forty-six percent of children in the United States ages 9 to 11 have cell phones as do 20% of children ages 6 to 8 (Bora, 2007). Even five-year-olds are getting into the act by using cell phones specifically designed for this age group, such as the Verizon Migo!

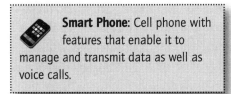

Smart Phone: Cell phone with features that enable it to manage and transmit data as well as voice calls.

COMMON OBJECTIONS TO CELL PHONE USE ON CAMPUS

Although increasing numbers of kids ages 5 to 18 own cell phones—presumably with parental permission—adults around the world object strenuously to these children being allowed to bring their phones to school. The Italian government banned cell phones on school campuses in 2007

("Italy Bans Mobile Phones in Schools," 2007). In January 2009, the Education, Science, and Technology Ministry of Japan urged primary and middle schools to ban student cell phones (Yamashita, Watanabe, & Uemura, 2009). And if given their way, the Pennsylvania legislature's House Bill 363 (February 11, 2009) will ban not just students' cell phones but any portable device that can record or play audio or video files on campus (Cruz et al., 2009). In other words, the legislators sponsoring this bill are so eager to prohibit cell phones that they are willing to ban virtually all forms of mobile technology—PDAs, digital cameras, MP3 players, laptops, tablet computers, and netbooks! Of course, this last example would represent a giant step backward for students in Pennsylvania and a groundswell of protest against this legislation is already growing among groups who object to the breadth of the proposed ban. However, it should be a source of concern that a law of this type has even been suggested. Why do cell phones raise so many red flags?

Mobile communication technologies have had negative connotations since paging devices became readily available about two decades ago, and then they were quickly adopted as the communication device of choice among drug dealers (Sims, 1988). Although no one claimed that pagers brought value to instruction, there were still objections when schools began banning these devices. For example, the American Civil Liberties Union (ACLU) argued that schools had legitimate reasons to ban pagers only when they created disruptions on campus, not simply because pagers had been linked to drug activity.

Educators and other officials still press for bans on these technologies. Three years after the New York City School District instituted an anti–cell phone policy that also prohibits use of pagers and other communication devices, the New York Supreme Court upheld the ban ruling that the ban does not infringe on student or parent rights. The judge who gave the decision cited incidents of cheating, sexual harassment, prank calls, and harassment as reasons for supporting the ban (Cheng, 2008). She also mentioned that when adults refuse to follow cell phone rules, it's difficult to imagine students being any more compliant. Parents who want electronic access to their children in a post–September 11 world have vowed to continue fighting the policy, but the abundance of examples of students misusing cell phones makes it an uphill battle.

CHANGING VIEWPOINTS

No responsible adult wants to promote cheating, **cyber-bullying**, or other misuses of cell phones. By the same token, it is important to recognize that

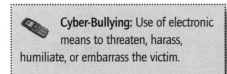
Cyber-Bullying: Use of electronic means to threaten, harass, humiliate, or embarrass the victim.

to younger members of our society cell phones are employed for far more than simply communicating via voice or text (eSchoolNews, 2006). Youthful cell phone owners use these devices as cameras, watches, alarm clocks, calendars, calculators, research references, and games. In fact, in late 2008, one-half of the titles included on the list of bestselling books in Japan consisted of novels originally composed on cell phones (Onishi, 2008). Based on this fact, some educators are learning that when they can get their students to view cell phones as tools instead of toys, it is possible to introduce classroom activities that are both engaging and instructive (Snider, 2008).

STRATEGIES FOR CLASSROOM USE

A private school in Australia recently piloted a cell phone program based on the premise that it's more important to measure modern students' abilities to *find* information than their abilities to *memorize* information (Devaney, 2008). Educators who subscribe to this paradigm shift are exploring various ways they and their students can use cell phones in class and away from school to support information literacy and content production. However, these educators recognize the need to lay some ground rules before launching activities supported by cell phone use. They also understand that doing this preliminary work teaches valuable workplace skills in **digital literacy** and etiquette.

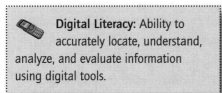
Digital Literacy: Ability to accurately locate, understand, analyze, and evaluate information using digital tools.

How often have you been annoyed by someone carrying on a loud cell phone conversation in a public place or using a cell phone in an inappropriate place, such as a restroom or theater? Do you regularly spot drivers who flaunt the law by engaging in on-the-road phone conversations or texting, becoming a menace to themselves and others? What about those occasions where meetings or services are disrupted by cell phones ringing or beeping? These are just a few examples of everyday misuses of cell phones among adults, and there are more. Photos are taken and posted online without permission. Harassing or threatening calls and text messages are made, or Web sites that are blocked on business or school computers are accessed using an Internet-enabled cell phone.

Students misuse cell phones in exactly these same ways. But how are they to learn better behavior without appropriate adult models who take the time to teach digital etiquette? Granted, parents need to take responsibility for teaching good manners to their children, but so do teachers and other school personnel who often spend more waking hours with students than do their parents!

But there's more at stake here than teaching manners. Just 23% of students surveyed for Speak Up 2007 believe that their schools are doing a good job preparing them for today's workplace (Project Tomorrow, 2008). Employers report that many high school and college graduates are ill prepared to meet the demands of today's workplace (Casner-Lotto & Benner, 2006). In each of these cases, a frequently suggested remedy is classroom use of technologies readily available to students outside of school, including cell phones. This makes it increasingly easy for educators to make a case that we owe it to students to encourage them to bring their cell phones to school to teach them appropriate and ethical use of these tools.

PRACTICAL SUGGESTIONS

How can cell phones be used to make a positive difference in behavior and learning? The New York Supreme Court judge was on target when she observed that even adults don't show basic good manners with cell phones. We need to begin by establishing and modeling ground rules for the use of cell phones in and out of the classroom. Liz Kolb (2008), educator and author of *Toys to Tools: Connecting Student Cell Phones to Education,* suggests working with students to develop contracts that establish expectations and outline consequences for misuse. Don't forget that contracts of this type must be reviewed by the school's leadership team or district officials to ensure they comply with existing policies and are enforceable. Students also benefit from direct instruction in digital etiquette. For example, teachers need to develop and use lessons that encourage students to anticipate potential problems with cell phone use and identify acceptable solutions to problems before they happen.

Once expectations are clear, teachers and students can use cell phones as tools for communicating and learning. As you plan lessons, remember to base them on meaningful learning. Do not use a cell phone in an attempt to engage students in activities that are marginally worthwhile regardless of whether technology support is built in. Here are some ideas.

Cell phone cameras: Students often find it easier to understand new concepts that are illustrated visually. Using the digital camera found on most cell phones, students can capture images that depict concepts they are learning. Even primary-age students can participate in this kind of activity.

Examples:

- Write and publish alphabet books illustrated with photos of real world objects that begin with each letter of the alphabet.
- Challenge students to find and photograph geometric shapes in real life or to illustrate word problems in a series of photos.
- During field trips, have students document critical concepts learned using digital photos.
- Use photos to inspire creative writing (prose or poetry).

To ensure success for this type of assignment, you need to have a place for students to upload their photos at school or from home. This can be a photo album or collection on a free photo-hosting Web site such as Flickr (http://flickr.com) or Shutterfly (www.shutterfly.com/) where access is limited to you and your students.

Podcasting on the go: Podcasts are audio files that teachers and students use for a variety of purposes. For example, teachers record podcasts for students to use when studying for a test or making up an absence. Students record podcasts to demonstrate understanding of a concept in various content areas. When podcasts first gained popularity, users needed a computer or laptop, a headset, microphone, and access to special software or a Web site to record and save the podcast. Now some cell phones have built-in voice recording capabilities. In addition, there are Web sites (e.g., Cinch at http://cinch.blogtalkradio.com/ or Drop.io at http://drop.io) where users call a special number using a cell phone or landline to record and save podcasts online. Students of all ages can create cell phone–supported podcasts.

Examples:

- During a field trip or lab experiment, students use the voice recording capability of a cell phone to save spoken notes.
- After completing an assigned reading, students use a cell phone to record and post their thoughts about the material or answer teacher-posed questions.
- Record interviews of school helpers, community members, or other people of interest using Cinch or a similar Web site. Post the results on a classroom Web page.
- Produce a weekly newscast for parents comprised of several short podcasts that offer various kinds of class and school news. Link the newscast to a classroom online site.

See Chapter 3 for an in-depth discussion of podcasting.

Online surveys: Personal response systems are popular among educators but not always affordable. Web sites such as polleverywhere (http://www.polleverywhere.com/) or MobiOde (http://www.mobiode.com/) make it possible for teachers to conduct quick polls, even short objective quizzes, where students provide answers using their cell phones. Free services are limited, but subscriptions are available starting at about $15/month. These activities may be conducted in the classroom or as a follow-up to a homework assignment.

Examples:

- Use a poll to teach a lesson on statistics and probability.
- Set up a poll to capture students' opinions about nearly anything ranging from how things are going in class to which short-story selection they like best.
- Create objective questions designed to measure students' prior knowledge of a topic before starting a new lesson.
- Write a quiz that students phone in after completing an assignment at home.

Research and study aids: Students and teachers may download study guides and other reference materials to their cell phones. In addition, it is possible to find answers to specific questions by sending text queries to Google and other online resources.

This chapter covers just a few of the reasons why cell phones have a place in the classroom. To learn more, review the entries in the resources section. You may also find it helpful to review and talk about the discussion points provided here.

DISCUSSION POINTS

1. How has your cell phone changed the way you communicate with others? Which features are most important to you and why?

2. Brainstorm a list of ways students in your school or district could use cell phones as learning tools.

3. Review your site or district policy related to cell phone use in schools. Decide whether the existing policy is suitable for a 21st-century learning environment. Explain your answer.

4. Create a list of at least three ways you can use a Web-based cell phone podcasting tool.

REFERENCES

Books

Kolb, L. (2008). *Toys to tools: Connecting student cell phones to education.* Eugene, OR: International Society for Technology in Education (ISTE).

Web Sites

Cellular Telecommunications Industry Association. (2008a, September 12). *CTIA: The Wireless Association.* Research-Harris interactive/CTIA survey. Retrieved from http://www.ctia.org/advocacy/research/index.cfm/AID/11483.

Cellular Telecommunications Industry Association. (2008b, June). *Wireless quick facts.* Retrieved from http://www.ctia.org/advocacy/research/index.cfm/AID/10323.

Cinch. (2009). http://cinch.blogtalkradio.com/.

Drop.io. (2009). http://drop.io/.

Federal Communications Commission. (2004, September 20). *The history of cell phones.* Retrieved from http://www.fcc.gov/cgb/kidszone/history_cell phone.html.

Flickr. (2009). http://flickr.com.

MobiOde. (2009). http://www.mobiode.com/.

Polleverywhere. (2009). http://www.polleverywhere.com/.

Shutterfly. (2009). http://www.shutterfly.com/.

Online Reports and Articles

Bora, M. (2007, August 26). Must-have for tweens: A cell phone. *St. Petersburg Times.* Retrieved from http://www.sptimes.com/2007/08/26/Business/Must_have_for_tweens_.shtml.

Casner-Lotto, J., & Benner, W. M. (2006). *Are they really ready to work? Employers' perspectives on the basic knowledge and applied skills of new entrants to the 21st century U.S. workforce.* Retrieved from http://www.conference-board.org/pdf_free/BED-06-workforce.pdf.

Cheng, J. (2008, April 23). Judge to NYC public school students: No cell phones for you! *ars technica.* Retrieved from http://arstechnica.com/gadgets/news/2008/04/judge-to-nyc-public-school-students-no-cell-phones-for-you.ars.

Cruz, Youngblood, Mustio, Caltagirone, Kortz, Reichley, et al. (2009, February 11). House Bill No. 363. Retrieved from http://www.legis.state.pa.us/CFDOCS/Legis/PN/Public/btCheck.cfm?txtType=HTM&sessYr=2009&sessInd=0&billBody=H&billTyp=B&billNbr=0363&pn=0410.

Devaney, L. (2008, September 23). Digital debate: Prepare kids for exams or life? *eSchoolNews.* Retrieved from http://www.eschoolnews.com/news/topnews/index.cfm?print&i=55284.

eSchoolNews. (2006, April 5). *Youths use cell phones as mini-PCs.* Retrieved from http://www.eschoolnews.com/resources/mobile-computing/mobile-computing-articles/index.cfm?rc=1&i=36915.

Italy bans mobile phones in schools. (2007, March 19). *Cellular News.* Retrieved from http://www.cellular-news.com/story/22649.php.

Kennedy, T., Smith, A., Wells, A. T., & Wellman, B. (2008, October). Networked families. *Pew Internet & American Life Project.* Retrieved from http://www.pewinternet.org/.

Kharif, O. (2008, August 28). Cell phones make headway in education. *BusinessWeek.* Retrieved from http://www.businessweek.com/technology/content/aug2008/tc20080827_832352.htm.

Olsen, S. (2008, July 15). For teens, the future is mobile. *Cnetnews.* Retrieved from http://news.cnet.com/8301–1023_3–9991979–93.html.

Onishi, N. (2008, January 20). Thumbs race as Japan's best sellers go cellular. *New York Times.* Retrieved February 15, 2009, from http://www.nytimes.com/2008/01/20/world/asia/20japan.html?_r=1&pagewanted=prin.

Project Tomorrow 2008. (2008, April 8). *Speak up 2007 for students, teachers, parents & school leaders—Selected national findings.* Retrieved from http://www.tomorrow.org/docs/National%20Findings%20Speak%20Up%202007.pdf.

Sims, C. (1988, September 25). Schools responding to beeper, tool of today's drug dealer, by banning it. *New York Times.* Retrieved from http://query.nytimes.com/gst/fullpage.html?res=940DE0DC1638F936A1575AC0A96E948260&sec=&spon=&pagewanted=all.

Snider, B. (2008, October 8). Learn21uvcell: A powerful multipurpose mechanism for learning. *Edutopia.org.* Retrieved from http://www.edutopia.org/print/5785.

Yamashita, S., Watanabe, M., & Uemura, S. (2009, February 1). Call for cell phone ban at school rings hollow. *Daily Yomiuri Online.* Retrieved from http://www.yomiuri.co.jp/dy/national/20090201TDY03105.htm.

MP3 Players   **3**

Some readers will remember when students surreptitiously listened to AM stations while doing their homework or smuggled transistor radios into class to listen to sporting events or music. Students today would laugh at the idea of risking detention or worse to use such a rudimentary listening device—and then slip an iPod into a pocket and discretely insert an ear bud to listen to a favorite music playlist or podcast. In short, adults and kids have often been at odds over technologies that allow users to listen to one thing while doing something else, with students vowing they can multitask and adults challenging that assertion.

Recently, the growing popularity of **MP3 players** among students has become the impetus for renewed discussion about this topic. Why are educators taking another look at the value of listening technologies? For one thing, this technology has taken the teen population by storm. In 2006, 54% of all U.S. teens owned *at least* one MP3 player that they used more than 16 hours per week primarily to listen to music or watch video ("Portable MP3 Player Ownership Reaches New High," 2006). Another difference is that users can control what they listen to by creating their playlists of favorite music and podcasts. And what really tips the scales is that many players support recording, allowing users to produce their own content. The capacity to create and listen to original content also makes MP3 players interesting to most educators.

> **MP3 Player:** A digital audio player (DAP) that is used to store, organize, and play audio files. The name "MP3" comes from the most popular format for these audio files.

This chapter explores MP3 players and their potential for instructional use, including creating and listening to podcasts.

MP3 PLAYER BASICS

MP3 players are actually **digital audio players** (DAPs) that are used to store, organize, and play audio files. The name "MP3" comes from the most popular format for these audio files. DAPs are also sometimes called **portable media players** (PMPs) because they support viewing images and/or playing video, but the public tends to refer to both DAPs and PMPs as MP3 players. That's a lot of acronyms! To avoid confusion, the term *MP3 player* will be used in this chapter. Popular MP3 players include the iPod (Apple), Zune (Microsoft), and Zen (Creative).

> **Digital Audio Player:** Also called a DAP, this device is used to store, organize, and play audio files.

> **Portable Media Player:** Also called a PMP, this device is used to store, organize, and play audio files and supports viewing images and/or playing video.

The MP3 file format was patented in Germany in 1989 by the Fraunhofer Institute, but the first portable MP3 players were not available to the public until 1998. Called **MPMan**, the players were initially sold in Korea, hitting the U.S. market a few months later. MPMan retailed for $250 and boasted 32 megabytes (MB) of **flash memory** (Topolsky, 2008). Today's MP3 players fall into two categories: hard drive or flash memory. Hard drive MP3 players offer more than 100 gigabytes (GB) storage and are well suited for holding large libraries of music, video, and photo libraries. These devices sport a variety of features and tend to be pricier than their flash memory counterparts, which can hold up to 64 GB. However, some experts predict that advances in flash memory could make hard drive MP3 players a thing of the past once flash memory surpasses 100 GB (Gideon, 2008). Screen sizes range from 2 inches to 4.8 inches (diagonally), and a variety of file formats are supported.

> **MPMan:** The first publicly available MP3 players, initially sold in Korea in 1998.

> **Flash Memory:** A kind of memory chip that retains information even without a power source. For example, USB drives use flash technology as do digital cameras. Devices such as MP3 players and netbooks may use flash memory to store data.

Every MP3 player comes with special software that enables users to download and manage files—some programs even allow users to transfer files directly from a file source (CD, TV, cable, or satellite converter) to the player without having to use a computer. MP3 players also offer different capabilities for recording and playing back user-created files, various accessories, and wide ranges on battery life. Prices start as low as $10 for 2 GB flash memory players but can be $500 or higher, depending on the features included.

COMMON OBJECTIONS TO MP3 PLAYER USE ON CAMPUS

For the first few years after MP3 players went on sale, there was not much impact on schools. In fact, MP3 players accounted for just 5% of U.S. sales of portable audio products as late as 2001. Things changed rapidly, however, and by 2006, MP3 players represented 88% of all sales of portable audio products (Cook, 2006). This amazing growth in MP3 ownership caught educators' attention sometime in 2003 or 2004 when the number of students bringing MP3 players to school increased noticeably.

In most educators' minds, MP3 players initially fell in the same category as transistor radios, the walkman, and portable CD players. As such, classroom use was often restricted or prohibited based on the premise that MP3 player are distracters. Parents and teachers expressed concern that students could not pay attention to teachers or concentrate on their work if they were listening to music. An interesting twist on this line of thinking occurred in 2005 when the principal of the International Grammar School in Sydney, Australia, decided to ban iPods on campus, arguing that students who were listening to MP3 players on the playground were isolating themselves from their peers and not interacting with the larger school community ("iPod May Lead to Isolation," 2005). But for the most part, these discussions were localized and low key.

Then in 2007, bans on MP3 players gained international attention when teachers and school administrators began discovering that students were using these devices to cheat during tests. Some enterprising teens had started recording study notes, formulas, and other tidbits of information that they saved in their audio libraries and listened to during exams ("Schools Say iPods Becoming Tool for Cheaters," 2007). As a result, educators around the world instituted zero-tolerance policies forbidding use of MP3 players on campus.

CHANGING VIEWPOINTS

By spring of 2009, school officials started reconsidering these bans. This is because—at least in part—of a recent shift in public opinion about the need for use of mobile technology in education. In his article, "Are iPod-Banning Schools Cheating Our Kids?" Mike Elgan (2007) writes that schools need to rethink continued use of unplugged curricula that rely on memorization. He suggests that instead of preventing their use on campus, educators need to focus on helping students learn to use MP3 players effectively and ethically to promote growth in critical thinking, problem solving, and workplace skills. In addition, there are growing numbers of successful instructional programs based on the use of MP3 players at school and at home (Firth, 2009).

For example, the *New York Times* reports that several school districts in New Jersey use iPods to help English language learners improve their skills in English, and so native English speakers studying Spanish and French can gain proficiency in listening to and speaking those languages (Hu, 2007). The *San Francisco Chronicle* describes programs in Missouri and New Mexico where middle and high school students use Zunes to extend their school day by downloading and listening to teacher-created podcasts designed to help students review concepts when they are on the school bus or studying at home (Fonseca, 2008). And in the United Kingdom, students learn about intellectual property rights as they use MP3 players to access digital resources in music, English, and geography classes (Paton, 2008).

STRATEGIES FOR CLASSROOM USE

Mobile technologies such as MP3 players provide opportunities for educators to teach skills related to digital citizenship and academic content. A huge issue surrounding the use of MP3 players is the illegal uploading and downloading of music and video files. Because most teens spend the bulk of the time they use their MP3 players listening to music or watching video, it's highly likely that they have used—or been tempted to use—illegally shared files. Educators need to seize this opportunity to teach students about intellectual property and copyright laws by modeling legal and ethical use of files as well as discussing ways that misuse harms artists, writers, and performers.

Cheating is another issue teachers can address. The most beneficial way to do this might be to redesign activities and testing situations that currently make it all too easy for students to cheat. For example, instead of asking students to parrot back disconnected facts, structure exams so students need to synthesize or analyze information to write an essay or create a product that demonstrates their grasp of important concepts. Mike Elgan (2007) suggests developing what he calls "the iPod equivalent of 'open-book' tests" (p. 2). He believes that using this scenario, students should be encouraged to download information to their MP3 players and then use that material during the test to answer questions that go far beyond rote memorization.

The possibilities for teaching academic content via MP3 players are limited only by the educator's imagination. Teachers can create libraries of existing files for students to download and review. These files may include music, speeches, audio books, and more. Or teachers can take a page from eighth-grade history teacher Eric Langhorst (n.d.), who regularly posts podcasts his students can use to review material covered in class (http://speakingofhistory.blogspot.com/).

Besides becoming consumers of existing files identified by their teachers, students can also become content creators. For example, they can dictate and record notes while working on research or on a field trip. Or they can create podcasts on topics ranging from classroom news to book reports to presentations.

PRACTICAL SUGGESTIONS—USING EXISTING FILES

You've probably gathered that there are thousands of existing files that can be downloaded and played on MP3 players. This is where many educators want to get started. You can find free audio and video files at Wikimedia Commons (http://commons.wikimedia.org/wiki/Main_Page) as well as free and low-cost downloads at sites such as iTunes (iPod specific format, http://www.apple.com/itunes/) or LearnOutLoud.com (http://www.learnoutloud.com/).

You might also want to listen to audio files posted on school Web sites, blogs, or wiki by teachers and students at all grade levels. Here are a few examples:

- Grandview Library Blog (http://www.grandviewlibrary.org/)
- Radio Willow Web (http://www.mpsomaha.org/willow/radio/index.html)
- Teachers Teaching Teachers (http://teachersteachingteachers.org/)

Additional education examples may be found on the Education Podcast Network (http://epnweb.org/) or the PodcastDirectory.org.uk (http://www.podcastdirectory.org.uk/).

As you review different files, think about ways you and your students could use these materials to expand or enhance learning activities. Which files are most enjoyable or engaging? How is your interest impacted by the

> **Aggregator:** An online service that allows users to subscribe to audio and video channels to access files to download for use on an MP3 player.

length of the file, the quality of the recording or video, the relevance of the material being presented? After sampling various sites, download iTunes (http://www.apple.com/itunes/), Juice (http://juicereceiver.sourceforge .net/), or another **aggregator.** Read the directions for using the aggregator, and then subscribe to a few RSS feeds. This enables you to synchronize the files to an MP3 player and listen to them anywhere.

PRACTICAL SUGGESTIONS—PODCASTING BASICS

Creating content that supports classroom instruction and can be replayed on an MP3 player is one of the most popular educational uses for these devices. The files are called podcasts. This term was coined by combining the words *iPod* and *broadcast.*

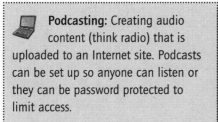

> **Podcasting:** Creating audio content (think radio) that is uploaded to an Internet site. Podcasts can be set up so anyone can listen or they can be password protected to limit access.

There are highly technical explanations of what **podcasting** is, but veteran educator and podcaster Steve Adams of Lopez Island, Washington, says the basics can be boiled down into two sentences. "Podcasting is creating audio content (think radio) that is uploaded to an Internet site. Podcasts can be set up so anyone can listen, or they can be password protected to limit access" (personal communication).

Originally, podcast creators needed to use a computer, a microphone, and a software program to record and save an audio file, typically using the MP3 format, which compresses sound sequences into a small file while preserving the integrity of the sound. Once the audio was recorded, it was edited and posted online. Depending on where the file was posted, it can be made available to a worldwide audience or just a few people.

Recording an audio file is a very different proposition today. Podcasters may use the recording capabilities of cell phones or MP3 players to record audio files. This introduces levels of mobility and flexibility that simply were not available until recently. Podcasters are now able to record files anywhere and then post them anytime they have access to the Internet.

Podcast listeners can access files in a couple of ways. Those who prefer to listen to audio files using their computers need an Internet connection and probably want to use a headset. To do this, all that's required is to be online and have a **media player program**, such as Real Player, installed on the computer.

Other listeners choose to download podcast files for later use. This can be done more than one way. To save individual audio files to the computer, right click on the file icon and

> **Media Player Program:** Software that is preinstalled on computers that allows users to listen to or view audio and video files stored on the computer. Real Media Player and iTunes are examples.

select "save target as" or "save link as." Or use an aggregator to subscribe to specific podcasts. When a subscribed podcast is updated, the new file is automatically downloaded, ready to be synchronized to an MP3 player or listened to on the computer.

Podcasting first caught the attention of postsecondary educators who began recording and uploading lectures that students could download and listen to on demand. But it wasn't long before K–12 educators began to see possibilities for podcasting with younger students. Besides making content available for students to download and listen to, teachers realized that students who created and published their podcasts were putting their literacy skills and content knowledge into action. This is because podcasting is not just a matter of sitting down with a recording device. Successful podcasts must be engaging and contain reliable information, requiring research, script writing and revision, rehearsal, legible recording, and editing before the podcast is published. Chapter 2 includes specific ideas for creating podcasts on the go using a cell phone. These same ideas can be implemented using an MP3 player with recording capabilities.

This chapter covers just a few of the reasons why MP3 players have a place in the classroom. To learn more, review the entries in the resources section. You may also find it helpful to review and talk about the discussion points provided here.

DISCUSSION POINTS

1. Do you own an MP3 player? If so, how do you use it, and if not, why not?

2. What is your site or district policy on student use of MP3 players on campus? Do you agree or disagree with this policy? Why?

3. Brainstorm a list of podcast topics for students and educators.

4. Think about ways you could use cell phone podcasting to communicate with other educators, parents, or students. How would this enhance home/school communication?

REFERENCES

Web Sites

Bonsor, K., Tyson, J., & Freudenrich, C. (n.d.). How MP3 players work. *How Stuff Works, Discovery Communications.* Retrieved from http://electronics.howstuff works.com/mp3-player.htm/printable.

Education Podcast Network. (2009). http://epnweb.org/.

Grandview Library Blog. (2009). http://www.grandviewlibrary.org/.

iTunes. (2009). http://www.apple.com/itunes/.

Juice. (2009). http://juicereceiver.sourceforge.net/.

Langhorst, E. (n.d.). *Speaking of history.* Retrieved from http://speakingofhistory .blogspot.com/.

LearnOutLoud.com. (2009). http://www.learnoutloud.com/.

PodcastDirectory.org.uk. (2009). http://www.podcastdirectory.org.uk/.

Radio Willow Web. (2009). http://www.mpsomaha.org/willow/radio/index.html.

Teachers Teaching Teachers. (2009). http://teachersteachingteachers.org/.

Wikimedia Commons. (2009). http://commons.wikimedia.org/wiki/Main_Page.

Online Reports and Articles

Carvin, A. (2007, May 1). The iPod of the beholder: Can MP3 players enhance learning? *Learning Now.* Retrieved from http://www.pbs.org/teachers/learn ing.now/2007/05/the_ipod_of_the_beholder_can_m.html.

Cook, B. (2006, August 2). Studies: MP3 player ownership highest among youth; accessories market hits $2 billion. *The Mac Observer.* Retrieved from http://www.ipodobserver.com/story/27825.

Elgan, M. (2007, May 4). Are iPod-banning schools cheating our kids? *Computerworld.* Retrieved from http://www.computerworld.com/s/article/9018594/ Are_iPod_banning_schools_cheating_our_kids_.

Firth, S. (2009, January 1). Schools attempt to redefine the iPod war. *Dulcinea Media.* Retrieved from http://www.findingdulcinea.com/news/Americas/2008/ December/Schools-Attempt-to-Redefine-the-iPod-War.html.

Fonseca, F. (2008, June 25). Rural New Mexico high school podcasts to students. *SFGate.* Retrieved from http://www.sfgate.com/cgibin/article.cgi?f=/n/a/ 2008/06/25/financial/f104505D84.DTL&feed=rss.business.

Forester, S. (2008, November 22). Boise teacher uses iPods in lessons. *The Olympian.* Retrieved from http://www.theolympian.com/northwest/v-print/story/ 670661.html.

Gideon, T. (2008, December 1). How to buy an MP3 player. *PCMAG.COM.* Retrieved from http://www.pcmag.com/article2/0,2817,2335605,00.asp.

Hu, W. (2007, October 9). In some schools, iPods are required listening. *New York Times.* Retrieved from http://www.nytimes.com/2007/10/09/education/ 09ipod.html.

iPod may lead to isolation. (2005, March 22). *News 24.* Retrieved from http://www.news24.com/News24/Technology/News/0,,2–13–1443_ 1679706,00.html.

Palenchar, J. (2007, March 12). MP3 player sales push record '06 audio sales. *Twice.* Retrieved from http://www.twice.com/index.asp?layout=articlePrint &articleID=CA6423469.

Paton, G. (2008, September 30). Children get lessons in iPods and downloads. *Telegraph.co.uk.* Retrieved from http://www.telegraph.co.uk/education/ 2689830/Children-get-lessons-in-iPods-and-downloads.html.

Read, M. (2007, February 7). Growing numbers of students use MP3 players as study tools. *Napa Valley Register.* Retrieved from http://www.napavalleyregister.com/ articles/2007/02/07/business/local/doc45c9e13a31a47296818650.txt.

Schools say iPods becoming tool for cheaters. (2007, April 27). *CNN.com.* Retrieved from http://www.iin.oea.org/2007/Noticias_pasadas_2007/ Noticias_mayo_2007/noticia2ingles.htm.

Topolsky, J. (2008, March 11). The first MP3 player celebrates its 10th birthday. *engadget.* Retrieved from http://www.engadget.com/2008/03/11/the-first-mp3-player-celebrates-its-10th-birthday/.

Press Release

Portable MP3 player ownership reaches new high. (2006, June 26). *Ipsos Insight.* Retrieved from http://www.ipsosinsight.com/.

Netbooks 4

In 2005, Nicholas Negroponte of MIT's Media Lab announced what appeared to be a nearly impossible project called One Laptop per Child (OLPC, 2009). His idea was to develop an inexpensive ($100) laptop computer for children living in underdeveloped countries around the world. This laptop would be small, rugged, require little power to run, have a full-size keyboard, a color display, and include built in Wi-Fi. He envisioned governments purchasing these inexpensive systems and distributing them to millions of children. By 2007, the XO was nearly ready to ship. Its price was a bit higher than the $100 target but still quite affordable. However, the story takes an unexpected turn here.

The OLPC laptops were not going to be available to the public. But ASUS, a manufacturer of notebook computers, started working on its version of a low-cost computing device that would be used primarily for accessing the Internet and checking e-mail. Released in late 2007, the original EeePC had just 256 megabytes (MB) RAM and a 2 gigabyte (GB) solid-state drive. But even with these limitations, the $299 systems sold out quickly. The surprise was that the tiny machines were snapped up not by residents of developing countries but by consumers in Europe and the United States who were looking for an inexpensive device that they could carry anywhere. Needless to say, ASUS responded to these sales by releasing a string of models, each just a bit more robust than the one before.

Although **netbooks** have taken off with adults who want an easy, inexpensive way to stay online, they are also popular with their original target audience—school-age kids. For example, two Japanese manufacturers, Kohjinsha and Bandai, have teamed up to develop a netbook specifically for primary-age children (Foo, 2009). Sales of netbooks in Australia account for more than 10% of all computer sales with retailers reporting that most are to parents whose children will use

> **Netbook:** Small-size, lightweight mobile computing device designed to easily access the Internet using built-in wireless capability. Most netbooks carry a low price tag.

the netbooks for homework and other school-related tasks (Moses, 2009). And older students are seeing netbooks as a viable alternative to traditional laptops for note taking and other less powerful but helpful applications in the classroom (Bajarin, 2008).

Let's take a quick look at this new class of mobile computing device and a few of the models catching educators' attention.

NETBOOKS 101

Manufactures and the media use a variety of names when referring to this hardware—**Ultra Mobile PC** (UMPC), **Ultralight PC** (ULPC), **mobile Internet device** (MID), **sub-notebook**, and **mini-laptop** are just a few—but *netbook* seems to be the current favored term. There are differences in these mobile computing devices; however, they share certain characteristics. All are small size, lightweight, designed to easily access the Internet using built-in wireless capability, and most carry a low price tag. Initial consumer reactions have been so positive that by 2008, nearly every major computer manufacturer had at least one version of these popular computers on store shelves.

Ultra Mobile PC: Often shortened to UMPC, this term is sometimes used to refer to a netbook.

Ultralight PC: Often shortened to ULPC, this term is sometimes used to refer to a netbook.

Mobile Internet Device: Often shortened to MID, this term is sometimes used to refer to a netbook.

Mini-Laptop: This term is sometimes used to refer to a netbook.

This is a rapidly growing market, with new product releases being announced regularly. Here are four netbooks currently garnering interest among educators around the world.

One Laptop Per Child (OLPC XO)

Launched in 2005, the mission for this project is "to create educational opportunities for the world's poorest children by providing each child with a rugged, low-cost, low-power, connected laptop with content and software designed for collaborative, joyful, self-empowered learning" (OLPC, 2009, ¶ 1). Credited with spurring for-profit companies to get to work on developing netbooks for the public, the XO laptops went into production in November 2007.

The XO was definitely designed for use under rugged conditions. Each machine can function as a wireless router, enabling children in remote areas to be part of what OLPC calls a mesh network. The wireless antennae double as external covers for two USB ports. The 7.5-inch screen display can be read even in bright sunlight and, unlike displays in conventional laptops, is designed to use very little power. The child-size keyboard is rubber membrane and the plastic case was created with harsh conditions in mind. For children with limited or no access to electricity, the computer can be solar or foot powered. The XO operating system is a version of open-source software called Sugar Linux.

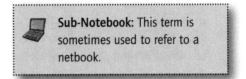

Sub-Notebook: This term is sometimes used to refer to a netbook.

Initially called the $100 laptop, the actual price is closer to $200 per laptop. OLPC originally targeted governments and ministries of education of the world's most needy nations as their priority customers. Two changes were made in this marketing strategy in late 2007. OLPC reconsidered its initial decision to prohibit U.S. sales. The foundation sponsored a promotion called Give 1 Get 1 (G1G1). Individuals in the United States and Canada were able to purchase two XOs at $399: buyers kept one XO for themselves, and the other was donated to a child in a third-world nation. The promotion initially resulted in sales of $35 million, but the second phase of G1G1 netted sales of just $3.5 million, so the program has been scrapped (Shah, 2009). In another shift from the original marketing plan, U.S. school districts in Alabama, New York, and South Carolina were permitted to purchase XOs for their students to start using in fall 2008.

But the worldwide economic situation is impacting XO sales. In an effort to get back on track, OLPC is no longer making individual or small-scale sales. Instead, the organization has returned to its initial focus—large-scale sales on a national level.

EeePC by ASUS

The three *E*s in this device's name come from its advertising slogan—"Easy to learn, easy to work, easy to play." The original EeePC was released in the United States in October 2007. Since then, Asus has launched several models. These compact units weigh up to 2.43 pounds. Screen size ranges from 7 inches in the earliest EeePCs to 11.6 inches in the most recent models. The keyboard is small—an issue for some adults but perfect for a child's smaller hands. Memory size runs from 512MB to 1GB. Storage in the earlier systems is limited, but three USB ports and a secure digital high-capacity (SDHC) card slot enable access to portable storage devices such as USB drives. All EeePCs have built-in wireless, speaker, and microphone, and most also have a built-in camera. The systems run either Linux or Windows XP operating systems. The later EeePCs are more expensive than earlier models because the display is larger, there is more RAM, the maximum storage capacity is expanded up to 160GB, and the battery life is extended. Pricing starts at $299 for the earliest models.

The EeePC is a nice system for students. The flash drive boots nearly instantly and the user-friendly, preinstalled interface can be figured out in minutes. Many schools originally opted to purchase the Linux-based models, which come preloaded with free open-source programs, such as Open Office and Firefox. However, now that XP is readily available, sales of these systems are growing. Just recently, ASUS released a netbook that will run Windows 7 and one with touch screen capabilities. EeePCs can be purchased online and in some retail stores. Take time to comparison shop online, and then contact vendors to discuss education pricing.

HP Mini-Notes and Mini 1000 Series

HP launched the 2133 Mini-Note in June 2008. Although this netbook has many positive features including a sturdy all-aluminum case, a 92% full-size keyboard, and storage sizes from a 4GB flash drive up to a 160GB hard drive, there are also some pitfalls. This netbook came with Vista installed and was extremely sluggish. In addition, the 2133 Mini-Note tended to get very warm while it was running. The recently released 2140 Mini-Note addresses these concerns, but a base price of $449 makes it pricey for a netbook.

HP's new Mini 1000 and Mini 5000 series may be a more inviting option for educators. There are currently several different configurations of these netbooks with pricing starting at $329. Minis can run Linux, but consumers may purchase machines with XP or Vista preinstalled. All feature an Atom processor, and additional air vents keep the netbook running cooler.

Mini 1000s are great for older students and adults. The display is easy to read and the nearly full-size keyboard facilitates typing. A quick online search will result in wide pricing variations, so be sure to comparison shop, and then talk with vendors about education pricing. The HP online store often offers deals not available on other retail sites.

Acer Aspire One

Acer entered the netbook market about the same time that HP released the 2133 Mini-Note. Models for this system are available in two generations and weigh between 2.2 and 2.8 pounds. The screen display is available in

8.9 inch or 11.6 inch, memory is 1GB to 2GB, and hard drive storage runs from 160GB to 250GB. Aspire Ones ship with an Atom processor and a keyboard that is 89% of full size. Three- and six-cell batteries are available. Both models include three USB ports; two SD card slots; and a built-in speaker, microphone, and camera. The systems run Linux and Windows XP operating systems. Pricing starts as low as $200.

With the slightly smaller keyboard, students may prefer this system more than adults. But the Aspire One is getting glowing reviews from both age groups. As is the case with the EeePC and HP netbooks, Aspire Ones are available online and in retail stores, but prices vary widely.

COMMON OBJECTIONS TO NETBOOKS USE ON CAMPUS

In talking with educators who oppose the use of netbooks on campus, there appears to be three primary areas of concern: network security, size, and system capabilities. The argument against allowing netbooks to access the school network nearly always comes from IT staff. It is true that opening the network to student-owned systems makes it more vulnerable to viruses, malware, and other forms of cyber-mischief. It is also true that one of the limitations of netbooks is that they are often running stripped-down operating systems, making it difficult or impossible to install add-on security software. As a result, many districts have policies in place that prohibit any use of personal laptops or netbooks on campus.

The second most commonly raised objection is size. There seems to be a direct correlation between the age of the person and whether size is a critical issue. Adults are most vocal about the small screens and the less than full-size keyboards. Secondary students express a preference for keyboards that are nearly full size, but they seldom complain about screen size. The youngest users appear to be quite comfortable with both—probably because the original netbook concept was designed with this age group in mind. The lesson to be learned here is the importance of piloting use of more than one kind of netbook before making a decision and being open to the idea of adopting more than one model.

Then, there is the debate about how much can—or cannot—be done on a netbook in terms of system capabilities. Linux does present a problem for less tech-savvy users, and some districts have backed away from purchasing systems running any version of this operating system. Another challenge is that Linux does not support many of the curriculum software programs teachers commonly want to use. Vista does not run well on netbooks either—it tends to be extremely sluggish. As a result, Microsoft has extended the "sunset" date for XP, meaning that most netbooks can now be purchased with XP installed. It remains to be seen how netbooks capable of running Windows 7 will fare.

Other objections raised focus on student need to run applications more powerful than those that can be handled on a netbook. Again, this is a problem only if netbooks are viewed as replacements for desktop or laptop computers, which they are not. Netbooks are designed to handle the kind of work that the majority of computer users spend the most time on—surfing the Web, basic word processing, viewing a brief video clip, and the like. When students have netbooks to handle these tasks, more powerful computers can be available to users who need them.

CHANGING VIEWPOINTS

Why does the burgeoning netbook market matter to educators? As increasing numbers of educators conclude that ready access is a key to effective technology use, interest in one-to-one computing initiatives is growing. But wide-scale, ongoing implementation has been hampered consistently by long-term costs. Low-priced netbooks make these initiatives feasible, making it possible to get more technology into the hands of K–12 students and their teachers. In addition, increasing numbers of parents are purchasing netbooks for their children, and they are pressuring schools to allow students to use these devices at school.

Educators and IT staff are engaging in conversations about how to make it possible for schools to provide these systems in large numbers and strategies for enabling students to use their netbooks on campus. One proposed solution is to set up guest wireless networks that students can access without endangering the main protected network. Another idea is to give students USB drives loaded with free antivirus and antimalware to install on their netbooks prior to being allowed to access the network. And offering professional development to teachers, students, and parents goes a long way toward protecting the network.

Some educators are also beginning to see that issues such as small size and limited capabilities can bring benefits. For example, the small footprint of netbooks means that it's easy for students to work on them at their desks and still have room for other instructional materials. The small size and light weight also mean that students can slip a netbook into a backpack or tote bag and easily carry it from home to school and class to class. And low power requirements mean that a six-cell battery actually can last all day without recharging. Finally, limited capabilities mean that is highly unlikely that students will be gaming when they should be working!

The true bottom line may come down to budget considerations. It's possible to purchase two or three netbooks for the price of one low-end laptop. With the current state of world finance, that fact alone may tip the scales in favor of netbook installations in schools.

STRATEGIES FOR CLASSROOM USE

Schools around the world are piloting use of netbooks with students in both elementary and secondary settings. Because these computers have been available for such a short time, most projects are still in their infancy; however, initial reactions from students and teachers are extremely positive. For example, Oregon School District located in Oregon, Wisconsin, initiated two EeePC pilots during spring 2008—one in a fourth-grade class and the other in high school English classes. Jon Tanner (2008), the district's technology director, reports, "Our pilot projects last year were successful, so this year we are adding the ASUS EeePCs as a supported project in our schools" (personal communication). He explains that this means that additional EeePCs will be available to high school English classes. In addition, the middle school and intermediate school have purchased EeePCs for student use, and all three elementary schools now have systems available to teachers.

HP 2133 Mini-Notes began shipping in June 2008, and the Fresno Unified School District initiated a plan to purchase and distribute 10,000 of the systems for use by second through 12th-grade students in fall 2008. The district initially piloted EeePCs, but opted for the Mini-Notes after students and teachers said they needed larger screens and keyboards at middle and high school levels. A full description of the pilot is posted on Microsoft's site at http://tinyurl.com/602fsr. Finally, the OLPC foundation sponsors a wiki that spotlights various XO pilot projects around the world. Visit http://wiki.laptop.org/go/Educators for more information about these programs.

PRACTICAL SUGGESTIONS

Experts generally agree that purchasing and installing equipment to reach a 1:1 ratio of students to computing devices is not enough to make a difference in academic achievement. For this investment to pay off, teachers need to rethink their approach to instruction by trying out student-centered strategies that focus on collaboration, communication, and problem solving. In short, although online research and word processing have their place, these activities are starting—not ending— points. What kinds of activities are well suited for support through a one-to-one initiative?

This question is trickier than it might appear. Teachers and administrators often think that *automating* an existing lesson is effective use of technology. On the contrary, although moving drill and practice exercises online or allowing students to type a report once it's been handwritten may engage students at first, the novelty wears off. And once it does, students resist automated activities to the same degree they resist the same activities in an offline environment. So what does work?

It may be helpful to link new ways of approaching instruction with familiar labels. For example, when imagining innovative ways for students to use technology, you can think in terms of project-based learning and constructivism. Both approaches are student based and rely on teamwork, supporting communication, and collaboration during and outside the school day. Here are a few content-nonspecific examples that can also be used to extend the school day when students have the means to work online at home as well as at school:

- Students create word-processing, spreadsheet, and presentation documents using Web-based applications suites such as Google Docs or Zoho. These files can be shared online with study partners or teammates for review, discussion, and simultaneous editing at school and at home.
- Provide a class wiki where students can post questions and provide assistance to one another related to any topic of study.
- Students use the built-in camera, speaker, and microphone to set up and record videoconference study groups or to interview experts in fields they are studying.
- Present several real-world problems to students who organize themselves into teams based on their interests and work to find a solution to one or more of the problems posed. When using this approach, students also become responsible for identifying the technology they will use during their work.

Since the first desktop computers were placed in schools, educators have struggled with how to find the money to bring in enough technology to make it worthwhile. Netbooks offer a realistic solution for this problem. If teachers at your site are not already familiar with this emerging technology, use this chapter to initiate the conversation.

DISCUSSION POINTS

1. Are you a proponent of one-to-one computing in classrooms? Explain your answer and provide supporting documentation for your argument.

2. What is your site or district policy on allowing students to connect to the school network using personal mobile devices? Does the policy need to be updated? Explain your answer.

3. Compare the benefits and drawbacks of allowing students to bring to and use personal mobile computing devices at school.

4. Is it reasonable to ask parents to purchase netbooks for their children? Why or why not?

REFERENCES

Web Sites

Acer. (2009). http://www.acer.com.

ASUS. (2009). http://asus.com/.

HP. (2009). http://www.hp.com/.

One Laptop per Child. (2009). http://laptop.org/.

Tanner, J. (2008, Aug. 11). EeePC Pilot. *TannerVision.* http://tannervision .blogspot.com/search/label/EeePC%20pilot.

Online Reports and Articles

Bajarin, T. (2008, October 17). Netbooks: Linux, Windows . . . or something else? *PCMAG.com.* Retrieved from http://www.pcmag.com/article2/0,2817, 2332657,00.asp.

Foo, J. (2009, February 10). Kohjinsha + Bandai = netbook for kids. *Cnet News.* Retrieved from http://news.cnet.com/8301–17938_105–10160573–1.html.

Moses, A. (2009, January 29). Netbooks hit right spot for schoolchildren. *SydneyMorning Herald.* Retrieved from http://www.smh.com.au/news/ technology/biztech/netbooks-hit-right-spot-forschoolchildren/2009/ 01/28/1232818513771.html.

Shah, A. (2009, February 24). OLPC to focus on large-scale deployments of XO laptops. *Network World.* Retrieved from http://www.networkworld.com/ news/2009/022409-olpc-to-focus-on-large-scale.html.

PART II

Web 2.0 Tools

Setting the Stage for
Chapters 5 Through 9

The term **Web 2.0** refers to the second generation of the World Wide Web, with a shift away from static Web pages and a move toward content that is dynamic and can be shared. Common Web 2.0 tools such as blogs, wikis, and social networks can be used to support collaboration and communication in virtually any instructional environment—when they aren't blocked by network filters.

Away from school, growing numbers of students are engaged in creating and publishing online content, gaming, and inhabiting virtual worlds. When asked their opinion, these students assert that the use of these tools in the classroom would make learning

> **Web 2.0:** The second generation of the World Wide Web with a shift away from static Web pages and a move toward content that is dynamic and can be shared.

more relevant and interesting. The following chapters explore some of these Web 2.0 tools and describe ways they might be incorporated into instruction.

Social Networks   5

W hether it's the local mall, a skating rink, a pizza parlor, or a nearby park, teenagers like to gather in places where they can hang out with their friends. But adults have made it increasingly difficult for teens to meet face-to-face outside of structured events. There are all kinds of reasons for this trend—parents of younger children object to loud, sometimes unruly groups of kids taking over a corner of a park and business people fear that these kids (who tend to spend limited amounts of money) drive off older customers who take their discretionary income elsewhere to make purchases. Parents express concerns about the safety of their own teens, alarmed by reports of smoking, drinking, and other illegal behaviors taking place at these gathering spots.

The mid-1990s saw a worldwide increase in loitering and curfew laws designed to allow adults to reclaim many public spaces by preventing kids from congregating in large groups. Here are a few examples:

- Daytime curfews based on the assumption that all kids under the age of 18 should be either in school or with their parents during the day.
- Evening curfews based on the assumption that these same kids should be home with their parents by 10 p.m.
- Mall curfews banning the presence of school-age children during the day or limiting teens' evening visits to those accompanied by a parent.
- Loitering laws limiting the number of unsupervised teens who can gather in a public location at any time.

Although it's tough to find an adult who doesn't agree that the world may be a quieter, more grown-up friendly environment with these restrictions in place, realistically speaking, when and where are kids supposed to be able to go to simply be with their friends? With increased focus on instructional minutes and time on task, nutrition breaks and recesses are a thing of the past at many schools, passing periods have been shaved to the absolute minimal amount of time needed to get from one class to another, and lunch periods have been cut to 30 minutes. That's okay, many adults think. School is for learning, not for socializing. But if teens can't socialize at school, and they are legally barred from those outside places where they used to socialize, where are they going to learn the social skills that once were acquired when kids hung out together?

In her April 2008, talk, "Teen Socialization Practices in Networked Publics," at the MacArthur Forum in Palo Alto, California, danah m. boyd (her spelling) argues that teens learn a great deal when they hang out with their friends.

> What does hanging out provide? First, social and emotional reprieve—downtime as well as support and validation. Second, potential introduction to new ideas and cultural artifacts. Third, and most importantly, hanging out is where youth learn to make sense of social norms, peer relations, and status. This is where culture is transmitted, interpreted, and reproduced. (¶ 15)

She believes that teens are turning to online social networks, at least in part, because they no longer have access to physical public space.

What exactly are social networks, and why are adults so concerned about what's happening there?

INTRODUCTION TO SOCIAL NETWORKS

Authors danah m. boyd and Nicole B. Ellison (2007) define social network sites as

> Web-based services that allow individuals to (1) construct a public or semi-public profile within a bounded system, (2) articulate a list of other users with whom they share a connection, and (3) view and traverse their list of connections and those made by others within the system. The nature and nomenclature of these connections may vary from site to site. (¶ 4)

In other words, these sites provide members a template for creating public and/or private profiles, a way to identify other members an individual might want to "friend," and make it possible to not only view a personal list of friends but also to look at friends' lists of friends—expanding the list of potential new friends. Each site structures these friend networks in different ways, but the basic idea is the same.

The idea of using computers to connect individuals with similar interests is not new. In the mid-to late 1980s, listservs and online bulletin board systems served this function. Consisting primarily of e-mail or threaded discussions, users could search directories of groups and subscribe to those on topics of interest to them. Listservs were very simplistic—get your e-mail address added to the group and start reading messages that arrived in your e-mail inbox. Bulletin board services weren't much more complicated, but they did usually offer a rudimentary profile option and, instead of receiving e-mail notifications, users navigated to the site where the threaded discussions were hosted to log in and read updates.

The mid-to late 1990s was a time of growth for social networks. Online communities such as Tripod and Geocities offered users tools to create and post personal home pages, often focused on specific areas of interest as well as chat rooms where members could gather to discuss topics. Classmates.com also launched in the 1990s. The purpose of this social network is to encourage people who attended school together to reconnect online. Basic members can create profiles, contribute to community message boards, and read other members' profiles, but to e-mail another Classmates.com member, a subscription fee is required.

The early 2000s saw the emergence of Friendster, MySpace, and Bebo social network sites. Friendster tends to be most popular in Asia, and Bebo has a strong user base in parts of Europe, but MySpace took the United States by storm. Many educators do not realize that MySpace originally targeted musicians. The idea was to provide an online community where composers and performers could share their work and discuss topics related to the world of music, but it wasn't long before MySpace became the social network service of choice for teens and young adults.

Membership is free—revenue to keep the site going is generated through ads placed on the site. Members create a profile by completing a template where they can add information "about me" and "who I'd like to meet," select emoticons to depict the member's current mood, and write blog posts. Personal profile pages can be customized by uploading photos or selecting from a growing number of page themes. Site features include groups, instant messaging, forums, MySpace TV, polls, and the ability to access and use MySpace from a cell phone.

MySpace was the top online social network site among U.S. teens and young adults until May 2008, when Facebook racked up 123.9 million unique visitors for the month, compared to MySpace's 114.6 million unique visitors for the same period (McCarthy, 2008). According to Web site use statistics published by Alexa, a company that tracks worldwide Web site use, Facebook is now the third most popular Web site in the United States, following Google and Yahoo.

Launched in 2004, Facebook was founded by Mark Zuckerberg and his roommates Dustin Moskovitz and Chris Hughes, who were all students at Harvard. Membership was originally limited to Harvard students, but it caught on so quickly that the network was soon extended to all university and college campuses in the United States. In 2005, high school students were invited to join, and by 2006, Facebook was open to anyone with an e-mail address. Facebook currently reports more than 175 million active users, more than one-half of whom are not college students with the fastest growing demographic being those over the age of 30.

Use of **social network services** had grown so rapidly that in a recent survey of worldwide social network users conducted by Nielsen, survey respondents reported spending more time on social network sites than on answering e-mail. The surprise in these findings is that the members driving this increase in use are not teens but people who are age 35 and older (Hachman, 2009)! This may mean that teens and young adults on the bleeding edge of technology use are already moving on to the *next thing*, but with millions of school-age users logging into social network services every day, schools will still need to deal with this issue for some time to come.

> **Social Network Services:** "Web-based services that allow individuals to (1) construct a public or semi-public profile within a bounded system, (2) articulate a list of other users with whom they share a connection, and (3) view and traverse their list of connections and those made by others within the system. The nature and nomenclature of these connections may vary from site to site" (boyd & Ellison, 2007, ¶ 4).

COMMON OBJECTIONS TO SOCIAL NETWORK SERVICES USE ON CAMPUS

It is difficult to think of a technology application that has been more heavily demonized than social network services. Just bringing up the topic in a room filled with educators, law enforcement officials, or legislators can unleash deeply emotional discussions about online predators, safety and privacy issues, and the amount of time youngsters "waste" in these online environments. And it is true that there are many examples of teens and tweens misusing social network sites. With 65% of all online teens having at least one social network profile, and 75% of young adults age 18 to 24 using these sites (Lenhart, 2009), it behooves us to make a serious effort to cut through the mythology that has sprung up related to the specific dangers of social networking services and attempt to identify those areas where adults should focus their efforts when helping teens and tweens learn ways to use social network services appropriately.

One of the most common voiced objections to allowing kids to use social network services is the presence of online predators. Statistics such as "One in seven youngsters have been approached by an online predator" (Wolak, Finkelhor, & Mitchell, 2007) are bandied about and basically used to shut down any further discussion about whether teens and tweens should be allowed to use MySpace or Facebook. However, the statistic— as cited—is not true. According to the researchers who conducted this study, the reality is that just two of the survey respondents were sexually victimized by someone they met online. Furthermore, just 4% of survey respondents reported aggressive sexual solicitations that included attempts to meet offline, and one-quarter of those came from another teen known personally by the victim. Additional statistics show that just 4% of teens were asked to provide a sexually explicit photo, and just 4% of teens were upset by these requests (Wolak, Finkelhor, & Mitchell).

The more accurate picture of Internet-related sex crimes is as follows. Most of these crimes involve adult men who use instant messaging, e-mail, and chat rooms to befriend teenaged girls. A very small percentage of these men pretend to be teens themselves (5%), and they do not hide the fact that they are looking for sexual encounters. Most victims go to face-to-face meetings fully anticipating that sexual activity will take place. Based on careful research, it appears that Internet-related sex crimes are nearly always cases of statutory rape that represent a very small percentage of overall numbers of cases of statutory rape reported annually (Wolak, Finkelhor, Mitchell, & Ybarra, 2008).

Online posting of personal information is another potential bugaboo. Most teens and tweens say they have been told they should keep certain personal information private, but again, there is little solid proof that posting this information endangers a student. One indicator that may make a difference though is the *type* of photos posted. Teens and tweens who post provocative photos are far more likely to receive sexually aggressive advances than those who post more chaste photos or no photos at all.

Does this mean there's nothing to worry about? On the contrary! Plenty of things kids are doing online need to be reined in, but educators have not paid as much attention to them as we should because they have focused so much time and energy on *stranger danger* issues. Where should concerned adults be directing their attention?

Cyber-bullying is an area that needs to be addressed. Forty-three percent of all teens who go online report being bullied online at one time or another, and three-quarters of victims can identify their tormentors (National Crime Prevention Council, 2007). A report issued by the Pew Internet & American Life Project in June 2007 (Lenhart) showed that teens who use social network services are more likely to be victims of cyber-bullying (39%) than are online teens who do not use social network services (23%). And some teens use social network services to harass adults by posting phony profile pages for teachers and administrators. In several instances, school suspensions—even expulsions—over this type of cyber-bullying have been upheld in court, often to the surprise of the student and his or her family.

Teens and tweens also need to understand that MySpace and Facebook are public spaces. It is increasingly common to read about students who are passed over for jobs, not admitted to the college or university of their choice, or who suffer disciplinary procedures at school because of things they have posted on a social network profile. Adults object to the inappropriate comments, photos, even music linked to MySpace and Facebook pages but seldom take a proactive stance by discussing these and similar issues prior to someone getting in trouble—when it then becomes a moot point.

CHANGING VIEWPOINTS

The number of adult social network service users age 25 and older has jumped 400% since 2005 (Lenhart, 2009). Many young educators now graduating from teacher preparation programs have used one or more social networks as students and see no reason to abandon this practice. And the majority of adult users are engaging in the same kinds of activities as young adults and teens—they want to stay in touch with people they know and socialize online. This may be why growing numbers of educators are willing to take another look at whether social network services have a place in education.

Educators also appear to be warming to the discussion of new workplace skills. This hasn't been an easy shift—after all, we are more than one decade into the 21st century! And perhaps it's taken the fiscal crisis of 2008–2009 to get us to sit up and take notice of the fact that the health of our future economy really does depend on the health of the worldwide economy. Regardless of the reasons, effective use of social network services does require many of the skills being touted as necessary for digital-age workers. For example, employers surveyed for the 2006 report, "Are They Really Ready to Work? Employers' Perspectives on the Basic Knowledge and Applied Skills New Entrants to the 21st Century U.S. Workforce" (Casner-Lottoa & Barrington, 2006), identified applied skills such as collaboration/teamwork, professionalism/work ethic, and critical thinking/problem solving as being in the top skills needed by today's workers. Educators can use social network services to help students hone these skills as well as basic skills, such as written communication.

Finally, the growing acceptance that technology skills are critical workplace skills is also changing the way teachers view technology-supported instruction and the use of Web 2.0 tools. For the first time since the survey's inception in 2003, 73% of teachers who participated in the 2007 NetDay survey stated that technology skills are important for student learning, and 68% reported using Web 2.0 tools in instruction (Project Tomorrow, 2008).

STRATEGIES FOR CLASSROOM USE

Prior to using a social networking service with students, educators need to check their site or district acceptable use policy to ensure that they will not be violating the policy. If social networking services are specifically prohibited, the next step is to meet with the site administrator to explain the purpose of the proposed activities and how they will benefit students. There are social network services that are K–12 education friendly. Here are two sites that some educators are using:

- Elgg (http://elgg.org/): This is free open-source software schools can download and use to set up their own in-house social networks. The upside is that users have complete control over the social network service. The downside is that it's necessary to have access to a server and someone with the skills to set up and maintain the site. One option is to pay a subscription to a third-party service to host the social network.
- Ning (http://ning.com): Ning is a service that allows users to create their own personal social networks. Very popular with teachers, Ning will remove ads on pages where group members are students in Grades 7 through 12.

Steve Hargadon (2009), founder of several successful education-related groups on Ning, says that building any kind of social network can be challenging. He points out that for a social network to succeed, several elements need to be in place. These include the following:

- Purpose: There needs to be a compelling reason to use the network.
- Focus: The online discussion needs to be interesting and to the point.
- Collaboration: Users need to feel free to contribute and create content that is not necessarily dictated by the network's developer.
- Moderated: The network developer needs to be engaged in the social network and sometimes will need to get conversation going or steer it in another direction.

PRACTICAL SUGGESTIONS

Although younger children can be successful members of monitored social networks, the target audience for this type of activity is most likely students in Grades 7 through 12. Some schools may permit teachers to use Facebook or MySpace, but it's more likely that most educators will need to use Ning or Elgg groups. It will probably be a good idea to begin by talking about *netiquette* and online presentation. Activity ideas could include the following:

- Build a profile that would be appropriate for both friends and a future employer to read.
- Use a rubric to evaluate an online profile from three viewpoints: student, parent, and employer.
- Provide students with a series of scenarios about online events (e.g., cyber-bullying, encounter with an adult who is a stranger, posting a message in anger) and discuss appropriate and inappropriate ways to deal with each situation.

Once students have demonstrated they understand appropriate use of social networks, explore ways students can use the social network for content-based activities. For example:

- A place for small groups of students to collaborate as they work on a group project where the end product may, or may not, be online.
- Periodically, an online game called a **meme** or tagging meme will sweep the Web. These memes usually include creating some kind of list and then tagging five friends so they need to complete the list. Students can create and share their own memes related to any content area.

> **Meme:** A catchphrase or concept that spreads quickly from person to person via the Internet.

- Create a profile for a historical or fictional figure. Choose a theme and populate the page with comments and images that represent this person. Be prepared to explain your choices.

Social networks are here to stay—at least for the time being. On their own, children cannot be expected to figure out how to use these sites appropriately, so educators need to help them. Educators also need to recognize that these sites can be a place where tweens and teens learn social skills and practice improving interpersonal relationships.

DISCUSSION POINTS

1. Describe your personal experience with social networking. If you have never used a social network, explain why.

2. What policies does your school or district currently have in place regarding student use of social networks? Are these policies working? Why or why not?

3. At what grade level should educators begin teaching students how to use social networks? Find documentation to support your answer.

4. Envision the role of social networking in 21st-century learning environments. Write a detailed description of this vision.

REFERENCES

Web Sites

Alexa. (2009). http://www.alexa.com/.
Facebook. (2009). http://www.facebook.com/.
MySpace. (2009). http://www.myspace.com/.

Online Reports and Articles

boyd, d. m. (2008, April 23). Teen socialization practices in networked publics. *MacArthur Forum.* Retrieved from http://www.danah.org/papers/talks/MacArthur2008.html.

boyd, d. m., & Ellison, N. B. (2007, November). Social network sites: Definition, history, and scholarship. *Journal of Computer-Mediated Communication,* 13(1). Retrieved from http://jcmc.indiana.edu/vol13/issue1/boyd.ellison.html.

Casner-Lotto, J., & Benner, W. M. (2006). *Are they really ready to work? Employers' perspectives on the basic knowledge and applied skills of new entrants to the 21st century U.S. workforce.* Retrieved from http://www.conference-board.org/pdf_free/BED-06-workforce.pdf.

Hachman, M. (2009, March 10). More time spent social networking than on email. *PCMag.* Retrieved from http://www.pcmag.com/article2/0,2817,2342757,00.asp.

Hargadon, S. (2009, January 28). Some things I've learned about building effective social networks. *Steve Hargadon.com.* Retrieved from http://www.stevehargadon.com/2009/01/some-things-ive-learned-about-building.html.

Lenhart, A. (2007, June 27). Cyberbullying and online teens. *Pew Internet & American Life Project.* Retrieved from http://www.pewinternet.org/~/media//Files/Reports/2007/ PIP%20Cyberbullying%20Memo.pdf.

Lenhart, A. (2009, January 14). Social networks grow: Friending mom and dad. *Pew Internet & American Life Project*. Retrieved from http://pewresearch.org/pubs/1079/social-networks-grow.

McCarthy, C. (2008, June 23). Facebook overtakes MySpace globally. *ZDNet News*. Retrieved from http://news.zdnet.com/2100–1035_22–207724.html.

National Crime Prevention Council. (2007, February 28). *Teens and cyberbullying*. Retrieved from http://surfsafety.net/Cyberbullying-Exec%20Summary-FINAL.htm.

Project Tomorrow. (2008, April 8). *Speak up 2007 for students, teachers, parents & school leaders—Selected national Findings*. Retrieved from http://www.tomorrow.org/docs/National%20Findings%20Speak%20Up%202007.pdf.

Wolak, J., Finkelhor, D., & Mitchell, K. J. (2007, December). 1 in 7 youth: The statistics about online sexual solicitations. *Crimes against Children Research Center*. Retrieved from http://cyber.law.harvard.edu/sites/cyber.law.harvard.edu/files/1in7Youth.pdf.

Wolak, J., Finkelhor, D., Mitchell, K. J., & Ybarra, M. L. (2008). Online "predators" and their victims: Myths, realities and implications for prevention and treatment. *American Psychologist, 63*, pp. 111–128. Retrieved from http://www.apa.org/journals/releases/amp632111.pdf.

Virtual Worlds   **6**

In the 1947 holiday classic *Miracle on 34th Street*, Kris Kringle says to Susan, "To me, the imagination is a place all by itself . . . a separate country. You've heard of the French or the British nation. Well, this is the Imagine nation." Children and teens have always been fascinated by imaginary worlds—this is part of the draw of the Harry Potter books, the Star Trek television series, even comic books featuring superheroes. Now this age group is flocking in droves (as many as 8.2 million in 2007) to a new kind of imaginary world (European Network and Information Security Agency [ENISA], 2008).

Once the fodder of sci-fi novels and shows, **virtual worlds** are becoming increasingly popular in mainstream applications. During the 2007–2008 television season, *CSI: NY* featured a two-episode special focusing on crimes committed in and out of Second Life. Then in June 2008, the Syfy Channel announced the launch of a project in which a virtual world will be tied directly to a new television program. Toy manufacturers including Mattel and Disney offer their customers access to online worlds designed to expand or extend real-world play. And in some instances, toy purchases are made specifically to gain access to a virtual world.

> **Virtual World:** A three-dimensional, graphic representation of a community that can be based entirely on fantasy or have roots in a real community.

But use of virtual worlds isn't limited to after-school entertainment. Besides being highly engaging, imaginary worlds provide environments where students can learn to make sense of the real world as well. Increasing numbers of educators are experimenting with using virtual worlds to engage students in a wide range of learning activities.

In his chapter "Imaginary Worlds," found in *Memory and Mind: A Festschrift for Gordon H. Bower* (Gluck, Anderson, & Kosslyn, 2007), John B. Black writes about the influence imaginary worlds have on learning in middle school students. Interestingly, he found that photos and animations have little impact on student learning, but students who could directly manipulate objects in animations learned better using a variety of problem-solving measures. Virtual worlds make it possible for educators to create environments where students can learn by manipulating objects in the environment to test hypotheses and see "what if?"

So what exactly are virtual worlds, and what is their place in classrooms?

VIRTUAL WORLDS BASICS

ENISA (2007) defines a virtual world as "a computer-based simulated environment intended for users to inhabit and interact via avatars" (p. 10). **Avatars** are usually two- or three-dimensional graphic representations of people or animals, and often, they can be personalized. A virtual world may be modeled on the real world but can also be based on fictional environments.

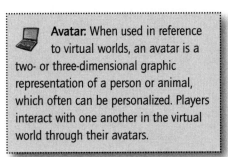

Avatar: When used in reference to virtual worlds, an avatar is a two- or three-dimensional graphic representation of a person or animal, which often can be personalized. Players interact with one another in the virtual world through their avatars.

In some virtual worlds, activities revolve around members assuming specific, predetermined characters while playing games built on these characters. For example, youngsters can create Barbie doll avatars in Barbie Girls (www.barbiegirls.com/) and then participate in various activities. Other virtual worlds allow members to alter their avatars, both physically and in terms of personality, whenever they choose and to interact with the environment at will. This second type of virtual world is not game-specific and is often called a MUVE (multiuser virtual environment). Teen Second Life (http://teen .secondlife.com/) is an example of a MUVE.

Virtual worlds are especially popular with children and teens. A company that aggregates and analyzes market data including Internet trends, eMarketer estimates that of the 34.3 million child and teen Internet users in the United States, 42% currently visit virtual worlds at least monthly. And it is expected that this percentage will rise to 53% by 2011 (Williamson, 2007). Companies that focus on the 3- to 18-year-old demographic are paying close attention to this trend. According to the Virtual Worlds Management Web site (2009), there are currently more than 200 virtual worlds either in operation or in development that target youth age 18 and younger. This list of sites, most recently updated on January 26, 2009, can be found at http://www.virtualworldsmanagement.com/2009/youth-01-26-2009.html.

Examples of Virtual Worlds

Virtual worlds can be grouped in a variety of different categories. In this chapter, we take a look at some of the better-known virtual worlds organized into two categories—those that focus primarily on social interactions and those intentionally designed for use in an educational setting.

Focus: Social

• Disney's Club Penguin (www.clubpenguin.com/): Club Penguin is a virtual world where members ages 6 to 14 play games, chat with one another, and engage in other online activities. Each member functions in the virtual world using a cartoon avatar that looks like a penguin. Basic membership is free, but members with paid subscriptions have access to additional options. For example, paid subscribers can purchase virtual items for the avatar's igloo or buy avatar costumes.

• Webkinz (www.webkinz.com): Said to be the first site to merge a real-world purchase with a virtual world, members ages 6 to 13 join this virtual world by acquiring a Webkinz stuffed animal that comes with a special code. When this eight-character code is registered online, the stuffed animal is "adopted," and the child gains access for one year to a virtual world where he or she can earn KinzCash by playing games, answering questions, and participating in daily activities. KinzCash may be used to buy food and clothing for pets, to furnish pet rooms, or to add to a pet's home.

• Habbo (www.habbo.com/): Habbo is a virtual hotel where teens use personalized avatars to socialize with one another. There are public areas where all members can congregate, and members can also create private rooms. These rooms can be furnished with virtual items, and members can adopt virtual pets. Online activities include games and social events. Membership is free; however, Habbo coins (20 cents each) must be used to furnish private rooms and purchase pets.

• Teen Second Life (http://teen.secondlife.com/): Developed by Linden Lab for teens ages 13 to 17, Teen Second Life is a virtual world where users interact in a three-dimensional environment. Once members create and customize their avatars, they can interact with other users or change and enhance the virtual world by creating objects, constructing buildings, hosting events, and more. The only adults permitted into Teen Second Life are Linden Lab supervisorial staff and educators who are working on special projects with students. The first basic membership is free, with subsequent basic memberships costing a one-time fee of $9.95.

Premium memberships are $9.95 per month, $22.50 quarterly, or $72.00 annually.

- There.com (www.there.com/): Teens age 13 and older may join There. This virtual world provides a place for teens to create an avatar, chat with other members using text or voice, buy and trade virtual merchandise, and build virtual homes. Members may also participate in online activities such as skateboarding or trivia contests. Basic membership is free and premium membership may be purchased for a one-time fee of $9.95.

Focus: Education

- Jumpstart (http://www.jumpstart.com/): Launched recently by Knowledge Adventure, Inc., the latest Jumpstart offering is a virtual world for children ages 3 to 10. Comprised of three age-appropriate areas, the virtual world consists of Story Land for 3- to 5-year-olds, Adventure Land for 6- to 8-year-olds, and Futureland for 8- to 10-year-olds. There's no charge to try the activities in one area of the virtual world, but to have full access, families pay a monthly fee of $7.99. This subscription covers all children in the family and provides access to Jumpstart's retail games. Parents can request periodic e-mail updates of their children's progress.

- SecretBuilders (www.secretbuilders.com/): In this virtual world, children ages 5 to 14 are encouraged to engage in a variety of creative online activities including playing games, caring for virtual pets, and interacting with one another. In addition, members may become content creators by publishing their writing, artwork, and videos online. There are no fees to join.

- Poptropica (www.poptropica.com/): Produced by the Family Education Network, the same group that owns FunBrain, and launched in 2007, Poptropica provides an online environment where children ages 6 to 15 may safely travel, play games, engage in competitions, and communicate with one another. Membership is free and the site contains no advertising.

- Whyville (http://www.whyville.net/smmk/nice): With more than 3 million active users, this award-winning site provides a virtual world where kids ages 8 to 15 explore a wide range of academic topics from science and technology to history. Project sponsors include well-known organizations such as the Getty Museum, NASA, and The Centers for Disease Control.

- Mokitown (www.mokitown.com/): Mokitown is a virtual world sponsored by Daimler and designed to help children ages 8 to 12 learn about traffic safety. Members meet one another as they travel safely through Mokitown, earning points that can be exchanged for extra privileges in the virtual world. Membership is free and the site contains no advertising.

COMMON OBJECTIONS TO VIRTUAL WORLDS USE ON CAMPUS

When it comes to using virtual worlds in the classroom, educators voice many of the typical fears and concerns that are expressed about most Web 2.0 tools. Here is a short list:

- Safety and privacy—How do you control who students come into contact with while they are online, and how do you monitor chats to ensure that students are not sharing private information?
- Cyber-bullying—Are members of virtual worlds likely to cyber-bully one another? How can this be prevented or dealt with?
- Inappropriate content—Are these virtual worlds safe? Is there a way to ensure that students will not be exposed to inappropriate content?
- Plagiarism and copyright issues—How do students know if work posted by other members has been posted legally?
- Advertisement and product placement—Are students being coerced into wanting to purchase merchandise they don't really want or need?
- Time spent online—Does membership in a virtual world encourage our students to become couch potatoes?
- Hidden costs for bandwidth and to upgrade equipment—Is it possible to ensure that students going into virtual worlds won't gobble up all of the network's bandwidth? Will the equipment currently owned by the school be able to handle the graphics?

Realistically speaking, it is impossible to guarantee that students will not run into one or more problems while in a virtual world. However, it is possible to take a proactive stance to reduce the risks involved. All reputable virtual worlds for children monitor online activity. Before taking students online, teachers should talk with them about how to handle themselves online. It is also helpful for the teacher to review steps for reporting other virtual world members who make them feel uncomfortable by asking inappropriate questions, using bad language, or through online bullying. Then, if students do encounter a problem, they will be prepared to handle the situation.

As much as possible, it's smart for teachers to stick to using virtual worlds designed for educational use. The one exception to this caveat may be Teen Second Life, if students are in middle or high school. This is not a guarantee that all content will be suitable, but it will help. Information literacy is an important 21st-century skill. Teaching direct lessons in strategies students can use to validate the authenticity of material posted online or to recognize information that has been copied from another source without proper citation helps reinforce information literacy. This rule of thumb should also help avoid student exposure to embedded commercial material.

It's unlikely that students will spend too much time in a virtual world during the school day. However, teachers may want to talk with parents about online use at home in general. In Symantec's second-annual Norton Online Living Report, an international survey of parents and students about online activity, parents estimated that their children spend approximately 18.8 hours per month online while their children stated it was more like 43.5 hours per month online (Kirk, 2009).

Technical issues, such as the availability of bandwidth and equipment capabilities, need to be broached with district IT staff prior to launching virtual world activities with students. Some virtual worlds such as Whyville tout the fact that they work well even on dial-up connections using older equipment. However, this is not the case with all virtual worlds, and these concerns can become serious issues.

CHANGING VIEWPOINTS

It is projected that 20 million children and teens ages 3 to 17 will be virtual world users by 2011 (Williamson, 2007). Although it is likely that much of this use will occur in virtual worlds designed to support social interaction, there is no reason why educators cannot capitalize on this interest to engage students in virtual learning activities as well.

The 2008 Horizon Report (Johnson, Levine, & Smith, 2008) identifies educational use of virtual worlds as one of six significant trends. The report mentions that there has already been a great deal of work done in this area at the postsecondary level, and it states that interest is growing in elementary and secondary education. Promising uses for virtual worlds include distance collaboration, scenarios, and simulations that spark critical thinking and creativity.

STRATEGIES FOR CLASSROOM USE

Prior to taking students into a virtual world, teachers need to check the school or district acceptable use policy to ensure that using this type of tool will not be violating any terms of the policy. Those teachers who uncover specific prohibitions related to use of virtual worlds need to meet with a site administrator to discuss their plans and obtain permission to move forward. It is also important that these teachers take time to work with IT staff to avoid issues that may arise because of the way the equipment is configured or demands that will be placed on bandwidth.

Teachers need to take the time to think carefully about the purpose for taking students into a virtual world. What kinds of activities will they engage in while there? Will the activity require use of a site like Whyville that has already created simulations for student use or use of a site like SecretBuilders that offers structured and unstructured activities? Teachers who are working with older students and decide to use Teen Second Life will be starting from scratch and will need to design all student activities from the ground up.

A variety of other questions need to be considered. Here are a few. Is there regular access to adequate amounts of equipment? Will these activities take place during the day or be part of a before- or after-school program? Do students have access to computers and the Internet outside the school day, and will they be able to work on activities away from the classroom? What type of final product will students produce?

It's not enough to read about various virtual worlds. Teachers also need to try them out. Nearly all of the virtual worlds listed earlier encourage parents and educators to visit the worlds using a guest avatar or by creating their own avatar. Teachers need to do this and take the time to make sure that the readymade activities are educationally sound and worthwhile or to ensure that teacher-designed activities are doable. It may be helpful to connect with other educators using virtual worlds. The Skoolaborate blog (http://www.skoolaborate .com/) is an excellent starting point, particularly for teachers who want to use Teen Second Life.

Parents must be informed about these activities and provided explanations of their educational value. It may be worthwhile to host a meeting to invite parents to visit the classroom and try some of the activities their children will engage in. Teachers should also plan to post regular updates on a classroom Web site or blog.

PRACTICAL SUGGESTIONS

Perhaps one of the most important reasons for using virtual worlds with students is that these are places where students can explore ideas and creativity. But students may need to spend some time learning the basics of creating and personalizing an avatar and navigating the virtual world. Teachers may want to spend time discussing topics such as the following:

• Online safety: Prior to creating avatars, talk with students about online safety. What factors do they need to keep in mind as they name their avatars and complete profile information? How will they behave when chatting with other avatars? What kinds of information should be kept private?

• Personal image: How will the avatar look physically? How will the avatar be dressed? How will the avatar behave? Why does this matter? Peggy Sheehy (2008), Instructional Technology Facilitator at Suffern Middle School in Suffern, New York, teaches her middle school students an entire unit on exploring body image in Second Life.

• Navigation: Conventions for moving about virtual worlds vary. On some sites, users simply point and click to move the avatar. Others require using arrow keys and mouse clicks to move from one spot to another. Some provide elaborate maps members use to identify a location and then transport to it by clicking on the name of the location or entering a code for the location. Have students practice so basic navigation doesn't get in the way.

Once students have created an avatar and are comfortable with navigating the virtual world, here are some of the kinds of activities they might engage in:

• Early research is showing that students enjoy virtual meetings and are willing to spend more time in a virtual meeting than in a face-to-face meeting. Teachers may simply want students, particularly those in secondary classes, to take their study groups online.

• Students using SecretBuilders can chat with avatars of famous figures including Shakespeare, Macbeth, Oliver Twist, and other historical and fictional personalities. Have students choose a famous avatar from those available on SecretBuilders, prepare an interview, and then report on their findings.

• Students using Whyville are invited to contribute creative writing, poetry, and other original work to the *Whyville Times*. Encourage students to publish their writing here.

• Teachers who have the wherewithal to purchase an island in Teen Second Life or who can join in on a Skoolaborate project will find that ensuing activities are limited only by their imaginations. For example, students can construct virtual environments that reflect books they are reading or societies they are studying. Veteran Teen Second Life user and educator Stan Trevena of Modesto, California, has students participate in an exchange program to get to know one another through a series of cooperative building projects and events—all in Teen Second Life!

Are virtual worlds the classrooms of the future? No one knows the answer to that question yet. However, it is fair to say that virtual worlds are impacting how students approach learning—in and of itself, this is enough reason for educators to familiarize themselves with these rapidly evolving online environments.

DISCUSSION POINTS

1. Have you ever visited an online virtual world? If so, which one, and what were your experiences there? If not, explain why.

2. Do you think that virtual worlds have a place in the classroom? Explain your answer and provide supporting documentation.

3. What does your school or district policy say about use of virtual worlds in the classroom? How could the policy be updated to reflect current tools?

4. Visit at least one virtual world described in this chapter and identify ways you could use this tool with students or colleagues. (If Teen Second Life were of interest, you would need to visit Second Life instead to get an idea of what's possible there as access to the teen world is very restricted.)

REFERENCES

Movies

Hughes, J. (Producer), & Seaton, G. (Director). (1947). *Miracle on 34th Street.* [Motion picture]. United States: Twentieth Century-Fox Corporation.

Web Sites

Disney's Club Penguin. (2009). www.clubpenguin.com/.
Habbo. (2009). www.habbo.com/.
Jumpstart. (2009). http://www.jumpstart.com/.

Mokitown. (2009). http://www.mokitown.com/.

Poptropica. (2009). http://www.poptropica.com/.

SecretBuilders. (2009). http://www.secretbuilders.com/.

Skoolaborate blog. (2009). http://www.skoolaborate.com/.

Teen Second Life. (2009). http://teen.secondlife.com/.

There.com. (2009). http://www.there.com/.

Virtual Worlds Management. (2009). http://www.virtualworldsmanagement.com.

Webkinz. (2009). http://www.webkinz.com.

Whyville. (2009). http://www.whyville.net/.

Online Reports and Articles

European Network and Information Security Agency (ENISA). (2008, September). *Children on virtual worlds: What parents should know.* Retrieved from http://www.enisa.europa.eu/doc/pdf/deliverables/children_on_virtual_worlds.pdf.

Gluck, M. A., Anderson, J. R., & Kosslyn, S. M. (Eds.). (2007). *Imaginary worlds. Memory and mind: A festschrift for Gordon H. Bower.* New Jersey: Lawrence Erlbaum. Retrieved from http://www.ilt.columbia.edu/publicATIONS/2006/IWB3.doc.

Johnson, L., Levine, A., & Smith, R. (2008). *The 2008 Horizon Report: Australia–New Zealand Edition.* Austin, TX: New Media Consortium. Retrieved from http://www.nmc.org/pdf/2008-Horizon-Report-ANZ.pdf.

Kirk, J. (2009, March 16). Survey: Families wise up to importance of online safety. *PCWorld.* Retrieved from http://www.pcworld.com/businesscenter/article/161344/survey_families_wise_up_to_importance_of_online_safety.html.

Sheehy, P. (2008, June 23). Exploring body image in Second Life. *RezEd.* Retrieved from http://www.rezed.org/forum/topics/2047896:Topic:7172?page=1&commentId=2047896%3AComment%3A7435&x=1#2047896Comment7435.

Williamson, D. A. (2007, September). Kids and teens: Virtual worlds open new universe. *eMarketer.* Retrieved from http://www.emarketer.com/Reports/All/Emarketer_2000437.aspx.

Creating Content—Writing 7

Social networking, the ability to reach out to people around the world who share similar interests, is a big online draw for kids and teens. But beyond social networks, there's another capability of Web 2.0 tools that is engaging today's students. The ability to create and publish online content in a variety of formats enables students, on a weekly basis, to spend significant time on creative purposes such as developing and maintaining Web sites, writing blogs, and posting articles. Here are a few statistics from a report, "Teens and Social Media," published by the Pew Internet and American Life Project in December 2007 (Lenhart, Madden, Rankin Macgill, & Smith, 2007):

- 64% of online teens and 59% of all teens have created online content
- 33% of teens work on Web sites or blogs for others (e.g., friends, groups they belong to, or class assignments)
- 28% of teens have created personal online journals or blogs
- 27% of teens maintain a personal Web page

Another report, "Writing, Technology, and Teens," also published by the Pew Internet and American Life Project in April 2008 (Lenhart, Arafeh, Smith, & Rankin Macgill, 2008), states that all teens write for school and 93% write for pleasure. This report also includes one finding showing that teens who write blogs are more-prolific writers in general than teens who do not blog. Yet 62% of school districts in the United States prohibit blogging during school (de Boor & Kramer Halpern, 2007). How could educators be leveraging students' interest in creating online content to engage them more fully in assignments for school?

This chapter and the next explore creating online content. Chapter 7 focuses on writing, and Chapter 8 looks at videos, photos, and other images.

WRITING ONLINE

The current reports on students and online writing typically focus on teens partly because some of these sites prohibit personal use by children younger than 13, but it's likely that their views reflect those of younger students as well. Online writing is manifested in a variety of ways both informal and formal. Informal writing formats include e-mail, texting, instant messaging, and posting comments on Web sites or in response to others' blog posts. Formal online writing includes text on Web sites, original blog posts, online articles, poetry, music lyrics, and stories written for e-zines or online newsletters.

Interestingly, the majority of teens do not view informal online writing, which is nearly always personal communication, as being *real* writing. And they are aware that it is not a good idea to mix texting abbreviations, emoticons, or other shortcuts, such as ignoring capitalization and punctuation, with formal writing tasks. Teens and their parents believe that effective written communication is an important life skill, but teens think that schools could do a better job of teaching writing (Lenhart et al., 2008). For example, teens report that most writing assignments range from one paragraph to one page in length, and they say this is not enough and that these assignments are not particularly enjoyable. They say they want to be challenged by interesting topics, high expectations, and write for an audience beyond the classroom. A majority of teens also state they want to spend more time in class writing and would like teachers to make more use of technology-supported tools for writing (Lenhart et al., 2008).

There are a number of free online tools that educators can use with students in response to these requests. Three types of online writing tools—blogs and microblogs, wikis, and Web-based word processors—are described here.

Blogs and Microblogs

A **blog** is an online writing tool that consists of dated entries posted in reverse chronological order so that the most recent entry appears first. Entries, which may be just text or include embedded links and images, may consist of a sentence or two or be quite lengthy. Blogs can be configured to accept original entries from one or more authors and to allow readers to publish comments about original entries. To ensure that inappropriate

Blog: Online writing tool that consists of dated entries posted in reverse chronological order so that the most recent entry appears first.

remarks do not appear, it's possible to moderate blogs so comments are reviewed before being made public.

Free blog-hosting sites first appeared in the late 1990s. These sites make it very easy for even the least technology-savvy user to create a blog Web site in just a few minutes using a template and series of simple directions. More experienced users can modify the templates to reflect individual preferences by adding images or rearranging the page layout. Blogs usually offer an **RSS feed** feature so that readers who subscribe to the blog are notified every time it is updated with a new post or comment to an existing post. Popular blog-hosting sites include Google's Blogger (http://www.blogger.com/), Edublogs (http://edublogs.org/), and Word-Press (http://wordpress.com/).

> **RSS Feed:** RSS is an acronym for really simple syndication. An RSS feed helps readers subscribe to blogs and other Web sites that are updated regularly to keep track of these updates and have handy access in one place.

Microblogging is a form of blogging that limits message length—typically to 140 characters or less. Microbloggers usually post messages using text messages, instant messages, or via the Web. These posts may be viewed by anyone or restricted to selected groups of readers, depending on how microbloggers set their preferences. Messages may include text and links to Web sites, audio files, or images. As is the case with blogs, microbloggers can individualize their personal pages using readymade templates or by uploading their own images. Microblogging first gained notice in 2006 but has grown in popularity since that time, particularly among teens and young adults. Currently, the top microblogging sites are Twitter (http://twitter.com/), Plurk (http://www.plurk.com/), and Jaiku (http://www.jaiku.com/).

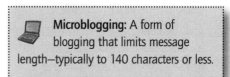

> **Microblogging:** A form of blogging that limits message length—typically to 140 characters or less.

Wikis

A **wiki** is a Web site that allows visitors to add, remove, and edit content. As is the case with blogs, wiki host sites provide templates that allow users to create a personal wiki in a matter of minutes. Depending on the wiki host site, it may be possible to individualize the template, but it is always possible to personalize the appearance of wiki pages by adding graphics and other online elements.

> **Wiki:** A Web site that allows visitors to add, remove, and edit content.

Public wikis such as Wikipedia, a Web-based encyclopedia, allow anyone to make changes and contributions. However, other wiki tools allow the wiki owner to limit visitors' ability to view and edit pages. Popular wiki host sites include PBWorks (http://pbworks.com/), Wikispaces (http://www.wikispaces.com/), and Wetpaint (http://www.wetpaint.com/).

Web-Based Word Processors

> **Web-Based Word Processors:** Applications that allow users to create, edit, and store files online and then publish these file on the Internet, when appropriate.

Web-based word processors eliminate the need to have special software installed on a hard drive to create a document. These tools are applications that allow users to create, edit, and store files online and then, if appropriate, publish the file on the Internet. Depending on the Web-based word processor being used, it's usually possible to upload and export files in a variety of formats (i.e., Word, Open Office, or pdf).

One of the most interesting features of Web-based word processors is the fact that they support online collaboration. The original creator of a file can invite others to view a document as a reader or as a collaborator with full editing rights. Simultaneous editing is permitted so two or more collaborators can work on a document at the same time. Popular Web-based word processors include Google Docs (http://docs.google.com/), Zoho Writer (http://writer.zoho.com), and Writeboard (http://www.writeboard.com/).

COMMON OBJECTIONS TO CLASSROOM USE OF ONLINE WRITING TOOLS

As is the case with social networking, many schools and districts have policies in place that either severely limit or completely prohibit the use of online writing tools and back that up with use of filtering software that blocks access to these sites on campus. Just 29% of school leaders believe that content creation using various online tools might have a positive impact on student writing, and 36% of school leaders believe that online collaboration can help students improve skills in teamwork (de Boor & Kramer Halpern, 2007).

Perhaps because they are best known and most popular with students, blogs are often targeted in school or district acceptable-use policies with some going so far as to prohibit personal blogs created and maintained at home outside the school day! School officials are appalled that teens use a public space like a blog to pour out their innermost thoughts and feelings, fearing that teens endanger themselves when they post personal information online (Kornblum, 2005). Another thorny issue is the fact that some teens use their blogs to post disrespectful or threatening comments about administrators, teachers, and fellow students. Comments of this type are nothing new, but in the past, they would have been made to a limited audience instead of being posted for worldwide consumption. Disciplinary actions taken in response have been upheld in some cases and denied in others, leaving school officials unclear on exactly what actions may be taken under these circumstances.

Microblogging is so new that many educators are not aware that it exists, let alone that students might be texting and posting messages during class. However, outside the classroom concerns are being raised about use of microblogging at inappropriate times. For example, television viewers were surprised by the number of Congress members who were busily posting comments to Twitter throughout President Obama's first speech to Congress. Officials in India were concerned that terrorists might read messages posted to Twitter during the Mumbai bombings to figure out what the police were doing to rescue hostages. And several mistrials have been declared because jurors were microblogging during the trial!

In general, fewer objections are raised to using wikis, but there are some concerns. Public wikis can be edited by anyone. As a result, unless they are closely monitored, these wikis can easily be vandalized by users who delete the work of others or who choose to add inappropriate comments or images. Many educators avoid this problem by avoiding classroom use of public wikis, choosing instead to create their own wikis where they can control who is given editing rights. This does not completely eliminate the problem, but it does mean that the wiki owner can easily track down vandals using the wiki history feature, which shows not only what changes were made but also who made them. In addition, by activating the moderation feature offered by most wiki-hosting sites, wiki owners are notified whenever the wiki is updated and are shown the edits that were made.

As is the case with wikis, there are fewer objections to Web-based word processors, although questions are occasionally raised about online security and whether documents are completely private. The main issue with these tools (and possibly with other tools described in this chapter as well) is the requirement to register using an e-mail address. The Children's Online Privacy Protection Act of 1998 (COPPA) prohibits asking children under the age of 13 for any personal information including e-mail addresses unless site owners are willing to do an enormous amount of paperwork in the process.

Some sites (e.g., PBWorks) avoid the problem by allowing teachers to create individual student accounts that do not require any personal information. Some sites (e.g., Google Docs) state that younger students may use teacher or parent-created accounts if the teacher or parent is present. This can be managed if every document is assigned to both accounts so students can work on a file at school or at home, but it can be somewhat cumbersome.

CHANGING VIEWPOINTS

Although tools that allow students to create and post written content online are still banned in the majority of school districts in the United States, attitudes are beginning to change. Parental expectations play a large role in this shift. The majority of parents in several recent surveys report they believe that when their children create online content, they increase both reading and writing skills. These parents also think that online collaboration, using tools like the tools described in this chapter, helps students learn to work with others.

School and district leaders recently surveyed state they are intrigued by the possibilities for online collaboration and providing opportunities for a variety of students to work together. These educators still want close adult supervision of students who are using these tools and are not interested in allowing access to chat rooms or instant-messaging services. However, the door is being opened and, if used thoughtfully, both teachers and students will benefit from use of these tools.

STRATEGIES FOR CLASSROOM USE

Before allowing students to create and post written content online, teachers need to check the school or district acceptable use policy to ensure that the use of these tools will not be violating any terms of the policy. Besides specific prohibitions related to the tools, there may also be restrictions on posting students' work. And teachers working with students younger than 13 need to read the terms of service for the tools they propose to use to make sure they will not be violating these guidelines.

Teachers need to talk with the site administrator before moving forward. They also need to have a plan that clearly demonstrates how instruction will be content-based and strategies that will be used to monitor students' use of various tools. These teachers may also need to work with IT staff to ensure that the sites are not blocked by the filter.

As teachers plan lessons, it's important to try out the activities to anticipate glitches that might arise. For example, when using a blog, the entire class will be able to reply to a posting at the same time, but when using a wiki, only one person can edit an individual wiki page at a time. If students need to work independently in a wiki, the teacher needs to determine if there is a way around the one-editor-at-a-time issue. This is also true when small groups need to complete work on a wiki.

PRACTICAL SUGGESTIONS

Using blogs, microblogs, wikis, and Web-based word processors is an excellent way to focus both on core content and on applied 21st-century skills. Before launching the first project with students, teachers need to spend time with students to review strategies for successful collaboration. It's important to not assume that students will know that they should not delete someone else's work without first communicating with that person or that students will know ways to make constructive, value-added comments on another student's work.

Teachers can set up conventions for students to follow as they work together. This may mean moderating comments on blogs and deleting inappropriate, hurtful comments or showing students how to use the comments feature on a wiki or in a Web-based word-processing document instead of changing text. Students also need to understand that wikis and Web-based word processors include features that enable teachers to track page and document history and to see every change along with who made the change.

Once behavior expectations have been set, here are some specific ideas for ways to use these tools for instruction.

Blogs

- Home/school communication: Some teachers use a blog in place of a classroom Web site. Assignments are posted in the blog and students are encouraged to post questions. Parents are also encouraged to access the blog to stay current on classroom activities.
- Book studies: This popular use of blogs encourages students to respond to writing prompts posted by the teacher as they read a book in class. Some teachers invite other classes reading the same book to join the conversation, and authors have been known to blog with students.
- Podcasts and presentations: Regardless of content area being taught, blogs can be used as an access point for student podcasts and online presentations (see Chapters 2, 3, and 8 for more information about podcasts and online presentations).

Microblogging

Teachers are experimenting with creating private groups on microblogging sites where students are encouraged to do the following:

- Respond to questions posed during class or post questions of their own.
- Write collaborative stories (see an example linked to the Many Voices wiki at http://manyvoices.wikispaces.com/).
- Communicate with class e-pals at another school. For example, second graders in Orono, Maine, recently used Twitter to write to second graders at another school.

Wikis

- Home/school communication: Teachers are also using wikis instead of traditional classroom Web sites. Parents and students can view pages to access class news, assignments, and resources. In some instances, students are allowed to edit specified pages of the wiki to upload work.
- Class projects: Nearly any project can be enhanced through use of a wiki that students can access at school and at home. Besides posting written work, students can upload related photos and embed podcasts and online presentations. Consider using a wiki for students to create a class glossary or a math problem solution guide or to document a field trip.

Web-Based Word Processors

Any written assignment can be enhanced through use of a Web-based word processor. Research shows that K–12 students who write using a word processor generally produce longer, higher-quality writing than students who write using a pencil and paper (Laitsch, 2003). In addition, the collaboration features of these online tools make it easy for students to work jointly on writing projects. Here are a couple of suggestions for working collaboratively.

- Round-robin writing: One student begins a story or poem and notifies the next student who adds a predetermined amount of text and then notifies the third student until everyone in the group has made the agreed upon number of contributions.
- Team writing: Groups of three to four students divide a writing assignment by subsection, each contribute their part, and then edit for flow and continuity.

- Peer editing: Using a predetermined rubric, students pair up, read one another's writing, and make comments/suggestions based on the rubric provided.

Engaged students tend to complete their work and do a better job than students who are resistant. Educators know that students enjoy creating content and posting it online. Capitalize on this interest to encourage students to write more, to write better, and to share their final products with an audience that extends beyond the walls of the classroom.

DISCUSSION POINTS

1. Explain the differences between blogs, wikis, and Web-based word processors. Identify one classroom activity for each type of tool.

2. What law might limit access to this type of tool to students age 13 and older? Was this the original intent of the law? What's changed?

3. Does your school or district have a policy about posting student work online? What does the policy state, and how does this impact use of the tools described in this chapter?

4. Do you have personal experience with any of these tools? If so, please describe that experience. If not, please explain why you have not used these tools.

REFERENCES

Web Sites

Blogger. (2009). http://www.blogger.com/.
Edublogs. (2009). http://edublogs.org/.
Google Docs. (2009). http://docs.google.com/.
Jaiku. (2009). http://www.jaiku.com/.
Many Voices. (2009). http://manyvoices.wikispaces.com/.
PBWorks. (2009). http://pbworks.com/.
Plurk. (2009). http://www.plurk.com/.
Twitter. (2009). http://twitter.com/.
Wetpaint. (2009). http://www.wetpaint.com/.
Wikispaces. (2009). http://www.wikispaces.com/.
WordPress. (2009). http://wordpress.com/.
Writeboard. (2009). http://www.writeboard.com/.
Zoho Writer. (2009). http://writer.zoho.com.

Online Reports and Articles

de Boor, T., & Kramer Halpern, L. (2007, July). Creating & connecting: Research and guidelines on online social—and educational—networking. *National School Boards Association.* Retrieved from http://www.nsba.org/site/docs/41400/41340.pdf.

Kornblum, J. (2005, October 30). Teens wear their hearts on their blog. *USA Today.* Retrieved from http://www.usatoday.com/tech/news/techinnovations/2005–10–30-teen-blogs_x.htm.

Laitsch, D. (Ed.). (2003, April 1). The effects of computers on student writing: What the research tells us. *ASCD Research Brief, 1,* (7). Retrieved from http://www.ascd.org/publications/researchbrief/v1n07/toc.aspx.

Lenhart, A., Arafeh, S., Smith, A., & Rankin Macgill, A. (2008, April 28). Writing, technology, and teens. *Pew Internet & American Life Project.* Retrieved from http://www.pewinternet.org/~/media//Files/Reports/2008/PIP_Writing_Report_FINAL3.pdf.

Lenhart, A., Madden, M., Rankin Macgill, A., & Smith, A. (2007, December 19). Teens and social media. *Pew Internet & American Life Project.* Retrieved from http://www.pewinternet.org/~/media//Files/Reports/2007/PIP_Teens_Social_Media_Final.pdf.

Creating Content—Images   **8**

Whether you call these learners *visual* or *spatial*, a significant number of students function best when they are permitted to use pictures, photos, drawings, and other graphics to organize and share information. Although they may not have as many opportunities to express themselves in school using visualization skills as they would like, these students have access to myriad tools outside of the classroom that enable them to create and share visual content online.

As early as 2005, one-third of teens surveyed reported that in addition to written work, they were posting photos, artwork, and videos online, and 31% of teens also said they regularly downloaded videos created by others (Lenhart & Madden, 2005). Similar percentages were documented in a report published in 2007 by the National School Boards Association. Broken down by media category, 30% of teens reported downloading videos created by others at least weekly, and 22% said they had uploaded videos they created. Nearly half (49%) reported uploading photos or artwork of their own (de Boor & Kramer Halpern, 2007).

The popularity of social networks and other Web 2.0 tools seems to support students' interest in uploading and sharing many different types of content. Chapter 7 looked at various ways students develop and distribute written material online. This chapter explores ways students, especially teens (age requirements on many sites may restrict use by younger students because of the **Children's Online Privacy Protection Act of 1998** [COPPA]), are using photos and video and strategies for using these skills in the classroom.

> **Children's Online Privacy Protection Act of 1998:** Also called COPPA, this act describes the kinds of information that may or may not be collected from children under the age of 13 when they are online. It also set out guidelines that Web site operators must include in their privacy policies.

ONLINE PHOTOS AND VIDEO

Digital Photographs

Kids of all ages love photography. Although cameras suitable for amateur photographers were first available in the early 20th century, it wasn't until after World War II when cameras became inexpensive enough that most parents could afford to put one in the hands of their children. Back then, there were inherent limitations on what kids could do with their cameras—the cost of film, flashbulbs, and processing as well as the fact that at least one other human being (the developer) would see the images being printed all served to keep young photographers in check. Polaroid cameras took the human developer out of the mix, but the cost of film and the fact that the photo could not be readily copied and distributed still meant that very few people were likely to ever see a particular photograph.

The first commercially available digital cameras appeared on the market in the early 1990s, and by 2001, digital cameras were being offered as an optional feature on some cell phones. Today, nearly every cell phone comes with a digital camera as a basic feature.

Initially, photos were downloaded to computers and printed on glossy paper, much like traditional snapshots. But it wasn't long before photo-sharing Web sites appeared on the Internet. At first, these sites treated digital photos like film photos. Pictures were posted, but site visitors were expected to purchase physical prints for viewing. These days, it takes just a minute or two to upload photos directly to a photo-sharing site, social network site, personal blog, or wiki with far fewer users actually making print copies.

Kids use digital cameras to document their lives, from family gatherings, to school events and activities, to time spent with friends. The number of photos they can take is limited only by the amount of memory in the camera, and depending on the type of camera used, photos can be published online or e-mailed to friends in seconds. In addition, many photo-sharing sites make it easy to edit photos and enhance them by adding frames, icons, or captions.

Digital Video

Home movies were the rage after World War II. But as was the case with still cameras of that time, the early technology left a lot to be desired. Movie cameras were expensive with additional costs for film, development, and projectors to view the films. In addition, it was often necessary to either splice together several short films or spend a lot of time between reels rewinding and threading the projector. The emergence of video cameras and camcorders made it easier for amateur photographers to shoot, edit, and view movies on videotape, but the development of digital camcorders made it possible for anyone to create videos. Increased access to high-speed Internet connections and video-sharing sites such as YouTube, Blip.tv, and Google Video enabled users to upload and share home video clips with the world.

Children and teens took to consuming digital video like ducks to water. A survey released in June 2008 by Nielson Online shows that kids ages 2 to 11 watch an average of 118 minutes of online video each month, and those ages 12 to 17 average 132 minutes viewing online videos per month. The most popular video-sharing site among children of all ages is YouTube (Nielson Online, 2008). And as mentioned earlier in this chapter, nearly one-quarter of online teens report that they regularly upload their own videos (de Boor & Kramer Halpern, 2007).

Ready access to digital cameras and cell phone cameras that support recording video and sound as well as inexpensive camcorders like the Flip Video Camcorder means that it's easy for kids to make their own movies. The Flip Video Camcorder even comes with software that allows users to upload video directly to YouTube and many other video-sharing sites.

Most studies on video creation and uploading focus on teens because of COPPA age restrictions. Why do teens post the videos they make? Mostly, it's because of the recognition they get from their peers as a result of their posts. Nearly three-quarters of teens who post videos online report they get comments on the video at least sometimes, and 24% say that people comment on their videos most of the time (Lenhart, Madden, Rankin Macgill, & Smith, 2007). So for the majority of teens, posting videos is a way to communicate with friends and start conversations—a way to get validation from their peers.

COMMON OBJECTIONS TO CLASSROOM USE OF ONLINE PHOTO AND VIDEO SITES

It's difficult to know where to begin a discussion of why educators object to students creating and consuming online photos and videos because there are so many different reasons! Students around the world have displayed some very poor judgment about what is—and isn't—appropriate to post or access online. These faux pas are often widely reported in the media, fueling arguments that students should not be allowed to engage in this type of online activity. The primary issues seem to center on privacy, safety, bullying, copyright infringement, and, recently, child pornography concerns. Let's work through the list as presented to briefly discuss each issue.

Privacy

It's one thing to shoot photos or video at a gathering of some sort to put into an album or share with a few other people. It's quite another thing to post these photos and video online. First, there's the question of whether the subjects of the photos/video know that the images are online and, second, if they consent to having their likenesses distributed publicly. Many people do not want to have their photo posted online for a variety of reasons—all centered on their right to privacy—and would not grant permission when asked. Many adults fail to get permission, so it's not a surprise that kids do not think to ask either.

One solution to privacy issues is to educate parents and students about the need to get the permission of every individual shown in photographs and videos prior to posting. Another option that can be exercised is designating photos and videos as private, available only to identified family members and friends. Teens actually do a better job of protecting photos than adults. Just 21% of teens say they never restrict access to photos while 39% of adults never restrict photo access. Both adults and teens are less likely to restrict access to videos, with 42% of adults and 46% of teens never restricting access to videos they post (Lenhart et al., 2007).

Safety

Although instances of online predators are not as common as the media would like us to think, it is true that students, particularly girls, who post their own photos are more likely to be approached online by strangers than are students who do not post pictures of themselves (Smith, 2007). And there are concerns that students can inadvertently share too much information through images in photos and videos that provide clues to geographic location or identity.

A second safety concern is that many people have posted inappropriate material online. Students can inadvertently access photos and videos that range from tasteless to pornographic on photo- and video-sharing sites. Although educators realize that students are using these sites away from school, they are concerned about liability and safety issues related to use of these sites on campus.

Several states now require that educators teach online safety lessons annually. This is a good idea, but educators need to think carefully about the approach they take. Lessons based on fear tactics are likely to backfire. It's important to be honest with students about why they need to take care online and to give them strategies for what actions to take when something does go wrong or makes them uncomfortable. The most important thing is to create an environment where students are comfortable coming to a responsible adult if they have a problem.

Cyber-Bullying

Of all the concerns raised by parents and educators, cyber-bullying (the use of electronic media to threaten, harass, embarrass, or otherwise bullying someone) is the most prevalent. When students get into difficulties online, it is more likely that they are being cyber-bullied than other safety issues put together. And in most cases, victims of cyber-bullies have face-to-face relationships with their tormentors.

Embarrassing photos and videos are common weapons of cyber-bullies, and students are as likely to target adults as they are fellow students. There are multiple, well-publicized examples of students using photo-sharing sites and social networks to post photos of friends misbehaving in a variety of settings. The same is true on video-sharing sites where students have posted video (shot using a cell phone) of teacher meltdowns or of fellow students engaged in silly, even harmful behavior. Fortunately, just 6% of teens report that someone else has posted an embarrassing picture of them without their permission (Lenhart, 2007).

Bullying is not a new behavior, but the ability to bully online takes the problem to new levels. Use of electronic media to bully means that victims can be targeted anywhere, anytime. Moving incidents of bullying online takes away all visual and aural cues, making it easier for bullies to persist in this behavior because they cannot see the reactions of the victim. More information including resources for educators is provided in Chapter 10.

Copyright Infringement

Digital media make it very easy for students to post material that has been copyrighted by someone else. For example, scanning a commercially produced photo and posting it online without the photographer's permission violates copyright. Another common infraction is posting a popular television commercial or segment from a program without permission. Hosting sites attempt to protect themselves by posting terms of service stating that the person who did the uploading is solely responsible when laws are broken.

Fair use provisions in copyright law do give educators and students more latitude than other users when it comes to instructional use of copyrighted material (see Table 8.1), but it's important to teach students about these provisions and how to determine when use of images or videos are protected by fair use. Every school or district should have a copyright policy in place. Teachers need to review this document with students. There are also good resources online, such as the U.S. Copyright Office (http://www.copyright.gov/) and Stanford University's copyright and fair use site (http://fairuse.stanford.edu/).

Table 8.1	Four Standards for Determining Educational Fair Use of Copyrighted Material

Fair use is not free rein. The law includes four standards to use when determining fair use, but it's left to the individual to make case-by-case decisions. As a result, there are no cut and dry answers. However, here are four questions teachers can ask themselves to help determine what is fair use.

1. **Is your planned use of the material noncommercial *and* instructional?**

   Your answer to this should be *yes* to both noncommercial and instructional.

2. **What is the nature of the material (i.e., nonfiction or fiction, published or unpublished)?**

   Use of published nonfiction more often falls under fair use than use of unpublished or fictional material because it's factual information that's readily available to the public.

3. **How much of the original work do you intend to use?**

   Excerpts are usually permissible, but there are limits.

4. **Does your use of the work negatively affect the copyright owner's ability to earn profits from the work?**

   Your answer to this should be *no*.

Child Pornography

Concerns about students posting sexually suggestive photos and videos are not new. However, recently both girls and boys have been taking nude and seminude self-portraits using cell phone cameras and e-mailing them to boyfriends or girlfriends who then e-mail the photos to others. Eventually, the photos are widely distributed. Called **sexting**, some officials are charging students who receive and send these photos with distribution of child pornography and other felonies. However, two-thirds of students who

> **Sexting:** The act of sending sexually explicit material, usually photographs, from one cell phone to another.

engage in sexting report they had no idea it was against the law. Clearly, educators, parents, and students need to address this topic.

CHANGING VIEWPOINTS

As is the case with tools that allow students to create and post written content online, many U.S. school districts ban photo- and video-sharing sites, but attitudes are changing here as well. Ubiquitous accesses to inexpensive cameras and camcorders as well as dramatically increased ease of use of photo- and video-sharing sites are factors. So are student and parent beliefs that online collaboration helps students learn 21st-century skills, such as communication and collaboration, media literacy, and life and workplace skills.

School and district leaders realize that students are bombarded with media when they are away from school. In fact, it's estimated that students ages 8 to 18 spend nearly six and half hours per day using various types of media—sometimes simultaneously (Rideout, Roberts, & Foehr, 2005)! Educators have long recognized that many students are visual or spatial learners who thrive in environments where they can demonstrate learning through visuals. In addition, use of images and video is a very effective way to reach English language learners. Couple this information with the fact that students find photography of all kinds extremely engaging and it makes sense for educators to identify ways to safely use the digital media tools at their disposal.

STRATEGIES FOR CLASSROOM USE

It is especially important that teachers investigate all school or district policies related to the use of photo and video and posting student work there. Besides rules about use of photo- and video-sharing sites, teachers need to familiarize themselves with existing policies related to copyright and posting students' likenesses online in any format. And as is the case with posting written work, if students are younger than 13, teachers must read the terms of service for the tools they propose to use to make sure they will not be violating these guidelines.

Site administrators must be kept informed by teachers who plan to have students post photos and videos and information about the instructional units or lessons should be shared with parents as well to ensure that all interested parties understand how this work relates to academic and media-literacy skills. It's also likely that it will be necessary to work with IT staff to ensure that the sites are not blocked and to ensure that there will not be issues with bandwidth when uploading large digital files.

Management strategies for projects of this type require careful planning. When students are creating content, how will the teacher ensure that students are aware of expectations for appropriate behaviors when working with digital media, have the photography skills they need to shoot good photos and video, and possess the technology skills required to upload photos and video and work with them online? Or when students are working with existing media, how will the teacher ensure that students do not waste a lot of time searching for online images and video, do not abuse copyright laws, have the skills to download and edit files, and handle any problems that might arise such as accessing something inappropriate? Although it's far more time consuming for the teacher, when working with existing media, it may be advantageous to go online ahead of time to create photo albums or download videos and ask students to make their selections from what's provided. Besides saving class time on fruitless Internet searches, this significantly limits the risk that students will be exposed to inappropriate material or misuse copyrighted media.

PRACTICAL SUGGESTIONS

Just as it's important to discuss effective strategies when collaborating on written work, it is also important to cover these ideas when working with media. Teachers cannot assume that students will know how to plan a media project or understand how to manage the project so that every team member pulls his or her weight. Yes, they will learn through trial and error, but because they will be online, it's best to deal with issues that can be anticipated before students get started.

Teachers may need to provide direct instruction in how to set up private photo- and video-sharing groups and then invite members to join. If the project includes commenting on work done by another student, it will also be important to take the time to discuss expectations for comment content. Teachers may need to moderate comments and delete inappropriate, hurtful remarks. Here are some specific project ideas.

Photographs

These projects can be developed using existing photos or by having students take their own photos.

- Photo albums: Make an album of photos that illustrates a concept. This can cover multiple topics in a variety of content areas, for example, geometric shapes found in real life, picture dictionaries, examples of gravity at work, historic sites in your town. Encourage students to comment on the photos in the album.

- Picture books: Young children can write for one another and older students can create stories for younger grades. Use photos to illustrate the picture book.
- Writing prompts: Choose visually rich photos, and ask students to write about them.
- Virtual field trips: Allow students to take digital photos while on a field trip and post selected images on your return.

Video

- Create a one-minute public service announcement.
- Make a video tour of the school for new students and post it on the school's Web site.
- Record interviews with community members. Interviews can cover a variety of topics from historic events to civic issues.
- Make three- to five-minute video tutorials about concepts taught in class. These videos can be used for review or shared with other students at the same grade level.

Online Presentation Tools

Once students have created a photo or video project, they will want to share their work. One easy way to do this is to embed photos or videos on a blog or wiki page. This allows students and parents to view the project without having to leave the classroom or school online site. There are a variety of online presentation tools that allow students to organize images and use templates to create slide shows that can be captioned or narrated. These sites are used by adults as well as kids, so close supervision is needed. Here are a few examples:

- Slide (http://www.slide.com)
- Comiqs (http://comiqs.com/)
- Glogster (http://edu.glogster.com/)

It's also possible to create online presentations similar to PowerPoint files using the Presentation tool in Google Docs (http://docs.google.com) or Zoho Show (http://show.zoho.com/).

Media literacy is a critical skill set for today's students. Educators need to help students become both effective consumers and creators of media.

Web 2.0 tools make it practical for teachers to incorporate instruction in these applied 21st-century skills.

DISCUSSION POINTS

1. What personal experience do you have accessing and viewing photographs and videos posted online? Have you downloaded photos or video clips to use in some way? Explain.

2. Do you have personal experience in uploading and sharing photographs or videos to the Internet? What has been your purpose for posting photos and videos online (or for not doing so if you haven't)?

3. Research your school or district policy on posting students' likenesses online. What guidelines are provided and, in your opinion, are they reasonable? Why or why not?

4. Find and record a definition for the term *creative commons*. Explain how the concept of the creative commons impacts teacher and student use of photographs and video clips created by someone else.

REFERENCES

Web Sites

Slide. (2009). http://www.slide.com.
Children's Online Privacy Protection Act (COPPA). (2009). http://www.coppa.org/.
Comiqs. (2009). http://comiqs.com/.
Glogster. (2009). http://edu.glogster.com/.
Google Docs. (2009). http://docs.google.com.
Stanford University. (2009). *Copyright & fair use.* http://fairuse.stanford.edu/.
U.S. Copyright Office. (2009). http://www.copyright.gov/.
Zoho Show. (2009). http://show.zoho.com/.

Online Reports and Articles

de Boor, T., & Kramer Halpern, L. (2007, July). Creating and connecting: Research and guidelines on online social—and educational—networking. *National School Boards Association.* Retrieved from http://www.nsba.org/site/docs/41400/41340.pdf.
Lenhart, A. (2007, June 27). Cyberbullying and online teens. *Pew Internet & American Life Project.* Retrieved from http://www.pewinternet.org/~/media//Files/Reports/2007/PIP%20Cyberbullying%20Memo.pdf.

Lenhart, A., & Madden, M. (2005, November 2). Teen content creators and consumers. *Pew Internet & American Life Project.* Retrieved from http://www .pewinternet.org/~/media//Files/Reports/2005/PIP_Teens_Content_Creation .pdf.

Lenhart, A., Madden, M., Rankin Macgill, A., & Smith, A. (2007, December 19). Teens and social media. *Pew Internet & American Life Project.* Retrieved from http://www.pewinternet.org/~/media//Files/Reports/2007/PIP_Teens_ Social_Media_Final.pdf.

Rideout, V., Roberts, D. F., & Foehr, U. G. (2005, March). Generation M: Media in the lives of 8–18 year-olds. *Kaiser Family Foundation.* Retrieved from http://www.kff.org/entmedia/upload/Executive-Summary-Generation-M-Media-in-the-Lives-of-8–18-Year-olds.pdf.

Smith, A. (2007, October 14). Teens and online stranger contact. *Pew Internet & American Life Project.* Retrieved from http://www .pewinternet.org/~/media//Files/Reports/2007/PIP_Stranger_Contact_ Data_Memo.pdf.

Press Release

Nielson Online. (2008, June 9). *The video generation: Kids and teens consuming more online video content than adults at home, according to Nielsen Online.* Retrieved from http://www.nielsen-online.com/pr/pr_080609.pdf.

Gaming

9

For thousands of years, people of all ages have entertained themselves by playing games. For example, there is documented proof that 6,000 years ago Babylonians played a board game that was a precursor to checkers or chess (History.com, 2009). Besides being an entertaining way to pass time, games are an engaging way to introduce or reinforce a variety of skills. Knowing this, teachers have leveraged students' interest in board and card games for generations. So it makes sense that with the advent of affordable desktop computers in the late 1970s and early 1980s, many traditional games were taken online. For instance, in the United States, the Minnesota Educational Computing Consortium (MECC) quickly became a well-known distributor of educational simulation games including *Oregon Trail, Odell Lake,* and *Lemonade Stand.*

Advances in hardware and the development of CD-ROMs led to more sophisticated online games for educational use. The late 1980s and early 1990s saw the rise of commercially developed software games that were both entertaining and skills based, including the *Reader Rabbit, Carmen San Diego,* and *JumpStart* series as well as simulations such as *SimCity.* But the world of online gaming has changed since then and educators have not necessarily kept up.

In 2006, 45 million American homes had game consoles (Klopfer, Osterweil, Groff, & Haas, 2009). By 2008, 97% of teens ages 12 through 17 said they played some type of video or online game, and 80% of these teens reported playing five or more different game genres. And despite the general stereotype of a gamer as antisocial male teen spending hours locked away playing games grounded in violence, overall, nearly as many girls game as boys, and the top two most popular game genres among teens are racing games and puzzles (Lenhart et al.).

Students believe that there is value in using gaming technologies in school. The top reasons they give are that games can be used to teach difficult concepts and that they are engaging. And growing numbers of teachers are expressing a willingness to explore use of gaming technologies in instruction as well. Ninety-four percent of the teachers who participated in the Speak Up 2007 survey said they see value in learning more about gaming (Project Tomorrow, 2008). With interest at these levels, games deserve a much closer look as an instructional tool. Although the following discussion encompasses both online and offline games, it does not include sports games.

THE BASICS ABOUT GAMES AND GAMING

The general structure of games—online or offline—makes them attractive to players of all ages. Interestingly, this structure closely resembles a well-designed lesson plan. For example, games have structure, provided through rules of play and clear objectives. Players get feedback throughout the game letting them know whether the strategies being used are helping to achieve the objectives. Games are built on one or more challenges and have an engaging sequence that keeps the player interested.

There are many benefits to playing games of all kinds, particularly when students are permitted to play without adult interference. For example, players take opportunities to experiment with various strategies aimed at achieving the objectives of the game. When a particular approach doesn't work, players learn from this failure and apply what they've learned the next time. Games that involve **role-playing** encourage students to assume different identities and try various behaviors to

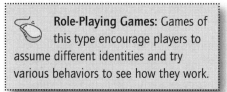

Role-Playing Games: Games of this type encourage players to assume different identities and try various behaviors to see how they work.

see how they work. Some games also allow players to learn about differing viewpoints, depending on the character or role they choose to play.

In his 2005 article "In Educational Games, Complexity Matters," Mark Prensky proposes that games can be sorted into two broad categories. He refers to the first category as **minigames** and the second as complex games. What's the difference? Minigames usually can be played in an hour or less and typically focus on one narrow topic. Multiple play levels may be available, but they are just more-difficult iterations of the same basic concept. Most educational games, both online and offline, fall into this category.

Minigames: As defined by Marc Prensky (2005), these games can usually be played in an hour or less and typically focus on one narrow topic. Multiple play levels may be available, but they are just more-difficult iterations of the same basic concept. Most educational games, both online and offline, fall into this category.

Complex games differ from minigames in a number of ways. These games usually require at least 20 hours to complete but may take 100 or more hours. Complex games offer multiple levels of play, each of which provides multifaceted challenges, goals, or missions that must be completed to move to the next level. Players are required to learn multiple skills, and many complex games must be played by teams.

> **Complex Games:** As defined by Marc Prensky (2005), these games usually require at least 20 hours to complete but may take 100 or more hours. Complex games offer multiple levels of play, each of which provides multifaceted challenges, goals, or missions that must be completed to move to the next level. Players are required to learn multiple skills, and many complex games must be played by teams.

Prensky (2005) writes that both types of games have their place in the classroom, but teachers tend to rely most heavily on minigames, not always understanding the difference between the two. This is because, aside from a few exceptions (e.g., bridge or chess), complex games have only existed for about 25 years, since computer technology made it possible to create games at this level of intricacy. Unlike their students, most educators have limited or no experience playing complex games, and they have difficulty understanding their potential value for instruction.

But in fairness to educators and other adults, even among youngsters, just 11% of gamers are considered "serious." These are daily players who prefer online games, own high-end equipment, and spend up to hundreds of hours on a game. The majority of gamers tend to be much more casual. They enjoy challenging games but prefer playing with family and friends, and they limit the amount of time they spend gaming because of other responsibilities, such as school. And the percentage of occasional gamers who prefer playing minigames for short periods is slightly higher than that of serious gamers (Klopfer, Osterweil, & Salen, 2009).

Video and online games are played using various devices. Currently, the Nintendo Wii, Microsoft Xbox, and Sony Playstation are popular game consoles. Nintendo's DS and the Sony Playstation Portable (PSP) are well-liked handheld gaming devices. In addition, minigames that can be downloaded and played in a few minutes are available for cell phones, **personal digital assistants (PDAs),** and MP3 players. Some minigames can even be embedded and played on social network and Web pages.

> **Personal Digital Assistants:** Also called PDAs, these handheld devices are used for a variety of purposes from managing calendars and contacts, to gaming, to basic word processing, and to using other work-related applications.

COMMON OBJECTIONS TO CLASSROOM
USE OF ONLINE AND VIDEO GAMES

Although offline board and card minigames have been learning-center and rainy-day staples for years, few educators made a sweeping transition to online or video games—even those that were nothing more than an automation of familiar offline minigames traditionally used in classrooms. Yes, some teachers purchased education games on CD-ROM or identified Web-based education game sites that students were permitted to access during class, but few provided PDAs or invited students to pull out their MP3 players, cell phones, or handheld gaming devices to play any type of game. In part, this latter scenario doesn't take place often because these devices are banned at most schools. But there are other objections as well.

Educators ask several common questions when raising concerns about most types of technology-based gaming in the classroom (Klopfer, Osterweil, & Salen, 2009).

1. What's the tie to curriculum? Educators want to know exactly how a game in either category relates to the curriculum they are being held accountable for covering and assessing. It's usually easier to see a direct tie to minigames than complex games because minigame objectives are so limited in scope. But the instructional value of minigames is also more limited than when students are able to dig into multifaceted concepts through complex gaming. There are complex games where the tie to curriculum is more readily evident. For instance, in games such as *SimCity* or *Civilization IV* players are challenged to build cities and empires from the ground up, which fits well in history and government courses. However, educators may have more difficulty connecting *World of Warcraft* or *Myst* to curricular goals and objectives.

2. How do children learn by playing? We tend to view learning as being a serious activity and are skeptical that children learn while they are playing. However, psychologists and child development experts disagree, saying that play is a very important part of learning. In addition, experts argue that children learn a great deal while playing online and video games: the skills needed to maneuver the game, the rules for the game, and strategies for playing the game are just a few of the critical-thinking and problem-solving skills kids can acquire. And when a game has a curricular tie, students can master content knowledge as well.

3. When am I supposed to find time to add gaming? This is one reason it's important to understand the difference between minigames and complex games. It may be that many teachers will still spend most gaming

time using minigames that can be completed easily in less than an hour, but the positive aspects can be enhanced when these games are chosen and used wisely. In addition, there is great value in challenging students to be game creators as well as game consumers. It may be that the most valuable use of minigames is to have students work in small groups to develop and share their online games. For those times teachers want to introduce more-complex games, they will need to consider scheduling playing time before, during, and after school. If using a Web-based game, it is possible that students can play from home as well.

4. How many times can you play a game before it gets boring? This is a minigame question, and it's true that some of these games are so limited in scope that they can be played just a few times before students have figured out the rules and strategies and are no longer challenged.

5. What about access to hardware? This is a serious concern in some schools, particularly if teachers propose using complex games. It's nearly impossible to engage in complex games using antiquated equipment with limited bandwidth or when the only access is in a lab. This brings up the possibilities raised in the first three chapters of this book related to allowing students to bring and use their hardware. Although it doesn't solve the bandwidth issue, it could help dilute concerns related to access to hardware. Researching what games can be played using which devices would take time, as would figuring out logistics for allowing student-owned devices to access school networks. However, it's not an impossible task, and with the support of IT staff and students themselves, a workable plan can be developed.

6. How do I assess skills learned in gaming? It's fairly easy to assess content knowledge acquired by playing minigames because of the narrow scope of these games, and the fact that they are often selected because they specifically reinforce certain curricular objectives. And because minigames take little time and are one of several teaching strategies in play, it's possible to continue to use the assessments a teacher would use anyway. Complex games are another matter. Although it's possible to measure content knowledge using a variety of assessment techniques already in place, many of the applied skills (e.g., critical thinking, problem solving, ability to work in teams) are not tested in traditional ways. Educators who want to measure growth in these areas are going to need to develop new assessment instruments, for example, rubrics.

7. How do I use games as tools for instruction? In many cases, the technology training attended by teachers is narrowly focused on basic skills and automating existing lessons and activities. Few teachers are

offered professional development opportunities to learn strategies for effective use of games as tools for instruction. And because many educators are not gamers, it's difficult for them to figure it out on their own, even when the interest is there. This is an area where the school administrator needs to make the commitment that professional development of this type will be made available to teaching staff.

CHANGING VIEWPOINTS

Other private and public institutions have used online and video games and simulations for training purposes for years. The U.S. military uses gaming to attract recruits, train soldiers, and recently as a tool for suicide prevention (Lubold, 2008). Medical schools use simulations to teach procedures, and a 2007 study shows that gaming surgeons have more dexterity than their colleagues who do not game (Stern, 2007), and companies ranging from Cold Stone Creamery to Canon use games to train employees (Jana, 2006). Authors and publishers are also exploring the value of tying books to online games. A well-known example of this is the 39 Clues series published by Scholastic. If the military, the medical profession, businesses, and publishers see value in gaming, it makes sense for educators to take a closer look as well.

As mentioned earlier in this chapter, there is growing interest among teachers in learning more about gaming in the classroom. This shift is not limited to the United States. For example, in a 2005 survey of teachers and students in England and Wales conducted by Ipsos MORI polls for Futurelab and Electronic Arts, more than half (59%) of the teachers surveyed stated they would be willing to use games in class ("Emerging Trends in Serious Game and Virtual Worlds," 2007). But where can an interested teacher get started?

STRATEGIES FOR CLASSROOM USE

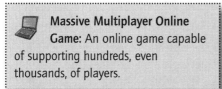

Massive Multiplayer Online Game: An online game capable of supporting hundreds, even thousands, of players.

Because this is new territory for the majority of educators, it's important to start small—it's not necessary to tackle a **massive multiplayer online game** the first time. Keeping in mind the differences between minigames and complex games, teachers should look for games that support content, offer multiple levels, and will keep students engaged over time. They also need to think about ways they might use the games to fill downtime or to extend the school day.

It's important for teachers to spend time becoming familiar with a variety of games using different devices, but it's also important that they try to enlist one or more colleagues who are interested in learning about gaming in classrooms. This will give them someone to bounce ideas off, and it also allows them to share their gaming research tasks and findings. Teachers might also seek out online communities of educators who have an interest in classroom gaming. One such community is Classroom 2.0, a Ning social network (http://www.classroom20.com).

Whenever teachers use games with students, expectations need to be established upfront. For example, when using a game where students choose a character to play, they can be challenged to choose different types of characters to compare points of view. Or when students use a simulation, they should not be permitted to simply guess what might work. Instead, students should be encouraged to think through a hypothesis before they test it or to do some research ahead of time. Finally, students need to be provided opportunities to reflect on their gaming experiences to be sure they understand the tie to content learning.

PRACTICAL SUGGESTIONS

Existing Minigames

Minigames can be used for up to an hour for a variety of purposes that range from giving students a quick break to practicing skills at multiple levels. If students download games specified by the teacher and then are permitted to bring an MP3 player or cell phone to class, they have immediate access to a gaming device during a break. For longer sessions, a number of free online game sites can be bookmarked on classroom computers or linked to a classroom wiki or blog to provide quick access when students are using a personal netbook or laptop. Here are a few links to explore:

- The Problem Site (http://www.theproblemsite.com/games.asp): Math games, word games, puzzles, and strategy games for Grades K–12.
- BBC Games Builders (http://www.bbc.co.uk/cbbc/): Games on a variety of topics.
- National Geographic Kids (http://kids.nationalgeographic.com/): Games on topics related to science and social science. Most appropriate for elementary and middle school students.
- High School Ace (http://highschoolace.com/ace/ace.cfm): Games for high school students including chess, Othello, and others.

Existing Complex Games

Many simulations are complex games. They encourage students to figure out how systems work and may require several hours to complete. It's usually easy to tie the skills students learn by completing a simulation to content being taught because they are often based on science or social studies concepts. Here are links to a few simulations that are appropriate for middle or high school students:

- *SimCity* http://simcitysocieties.ea.com/index.php
- *Spore* http://www.spore.com
- *CivWorld* http://civworld.gameslearningsociety.org/
- *PeaceMaker* http://www.peacemakergame.com/

Student-Created Games

One effective strategy for using gaming in classrooms is to have students develop online games. Small teams of students can create minigames in two to three hours, and development of a complex game can be coordinated as a semester or even yearlong project. One approach for doing this is to have students develop a storyline for the complex game and then develop levels for this game as minigames that are connected by storyline and characters.

There are online tools students can use for a project of this type including Alice (http://www.alice.org/), Game Maker (http://www.yoyogames.com/make), and Simple (http://www.simplecodeworks.com/website.html).

Children and teens enjoy online and video gaming at many levels and believe that its use in school would enhance their learning. Educators are now willing to rethink their doubts about the value of these games. As we work to find ways to engage students and keep them in school, it appears that now is the time to take a serious look at the role of online and video games in schools.

DISCUSSION POINTS

1. Based on personal observation, estimate the ratio of minigames to complex games currently used by students in your classroom or school. Which type is more prevalent? Why do you suppose this is the case?

2. What are your personal beliefs about the educational value of games? Please provide evidence that supports your opinion.

3. Conduct an informal poll of students at a school site to find out how many of them are gamers, the type of games they prefer, and their ideas about the value of gaming during the school day. Summarize the survey results. What did you learn?

4. What might be the value in having children develop their own minigames as an assignment? Explain.

REFERENCES

Web Sites

Alice. (2009). http://www.alice.org/.

CivWorld. (2009). http://civworld.gameslearningsociety.org/.

Classroom 2.0. (2009). www.classroom20.com/.

Education Arcade. (2009). http://www.educationarcade.org/.

Futurelab. (2009). *Teaching with games.* http://www.futurelab.org.uk/projects/teaching-with-games/.

Game Maker: YoYo Games. (2009). http://www.yoyogames.com/make.

GamesParentsTeachers.com. (2009). http://www.gamesparentsteachers.com/.

History.com. (2009). *History of toys timeline.* http://www.history.com/content/toys/timeline.

North American Simulation and Gaming Association (NASAGA). (2009). http://www.nasaga.org/.

Simple (2009). *Free programming language for kids.* http://www.simplecode works.com/website.html.

Online Reports and Articles

Emerging Technologies for Learning (Volume 2). (2007). *Becta.* Retrieved from http://partners.becta.org.uk/page_documents/research/emerging_techno logies07_chapter5.pdf.

Jana, R. (2006, March 27). On-the-job video gaming. *Business Week.* Retrieved from http://www.businessweek.com/magazine/content/06_13/b3977062.htm.

Klopfer, E., Osterweil, S., Groff, J., & Haas, J. (2009). The instructional power of digital games, social networking, simulations, and how teachers can leverage them. *The Education Arcade, Massachusetts Institute of Technology.* Retrieved from http://education.mit.edu/papers/GamesSimsSoc Nets_EdArcade.pdf.

Klopfer, E., Osterweil, S., & Salen, K. (2009). Moving learning games forward: Obstacles, opportunities, and openness. *The Education Arcade, Massachusetts Institute of Technology.* Retrieved from http://education.mit.edu/papers/MovingLearningGamesForward_EdArcade.pdf.

Lenhart, A., Kahne, J., Middaugh, E., Rankin Macgill, A., Evans, C., & Vitak, J. (2008, September 16). Teens, video games, and civics. *Pew Internet & American Life*

Project. Retrieved from http://www.pewinternet.org/~/media//Files/Reports/ 2008/PIP_Teens_Games_and_Civics_Report_FINAL.pdf.

Lubold, G. (2008, November 26). The army uses video games in suicide prevention. *The Christian Science Monitor.* Retrieved from http://www.csmonitor .com/2008/1126/p02s01-usmi.html.

Prensky, M. (2005). In educational games, complexity matters. Retrieved from http://www.marcprensky.com/writing/Prensky-Complexity_Matters.pdf.

Project Tomorrow. (2008, April 8). *Speak up 2007 for students, teachers, parents & school leaders—Selected national findings.* Retrieved from http://www.tomorrow .org/docs/National%20Findings%20Speak%20Up%202007.pdf.

Stern, A. (2007, February 19). Surgeons who play video games more skilled— U.S. study. *Reuters.* Retrieved from http://www.alertnet.org/thenews/news desk/N2J303978.htm.

Wilson, L. (2009, January). Best practices for using games and simulations in the classroom: Guidelines for K–12 educators. *Software and Information Industry Association (SIIA).* Retrieved from http://www.siia.net/education/foreducators/ games_final.pdf.

PART III

Digital Citizenship and Decision- Making Model

Setting the Stage for
Chapters 10 and 11

The previous chapters in this book include discussions about common objections raised when educators consider using specific mobile technologies or Web 2.0 tools. Chapters 10 and 11 provide strategies for making well-reasoned decisions about instructional use of mobile technologies and Web 2.0. Chapter 10 focuses on teaching and modeling legal and ethical uses of technology. Chapter 11 explores the critical relationship between educators and IT staff and provides a decision-making and implementation model that encourages educators to work collaboratively in grade level or departmental teams, as members of site or district technology committees, or as members of instruction review teams to carefully consider each emerging technology based on its merits and potential for classroom use.

Digital Citizenship **10**

Do you remember the song "Kids" from the 1960 musical *Bye, Bye Birdie?* As they sing, the parents of the show's ingénue lament the state of modern kids. Educators and parents often express frustration with today's kids and how they've changed. In reality, most kids *are* like we were at their ages. They want the same things we wanted: friends, validation from people they care about, and room to explore who they are and try different roles. They are making many of the same mistakes we made and celebrating the same kinds of successes we honored. What's different is the world they must navigate throughout this process.

When most readers of this book were growing up, it was possible for kids to make mistakes without drawing worldwide attention. Students could write and pass notes that said silly or unkind things, but the audience was limited to whoever handled the paper. Inappropriate photographs have been a part of teen culture since cameras, film, and the development process were affordable for the public. But the distribution of those photographs was limited. Bullies existed but needed to have close proximity to their victims to effectively harass or embarrass them. It was possible to plagiarize a paper or get a copy of a test, but doing so required a certain amount of work. Today, these and other negative behaviors are made easy by ubiquitous access to a variety of technologies that make it a breeze to post notes, photos, copies of exams, and more for global consumption. Within a decade, technology has significantly upped the ante for the cost of making a childish mistake.

This means that the adults who deal with these kids must rethink the strategies they use while parenting and teaching. And technology use is one area where many adults have serious knowledge gaps. There is so much to learn, and things change so quickly; it's difficult to keep up. The media sensationalizes kids' misuse of technology but rarely points out all the positive ways students are using technology, making it appear that most, if not all, kids are abusing it in some fashion. In frustration, parents sometimes ignore the situation or go completely overboard and severely curtail home use of technology.

Educators also tend to rely on negative solutions to technology use in schools. For example, because schools and districts depend heavily on federal funding to provide equipment and online access, schools agree to filtering requirements so stringent that they impede serious academic work. This situation is further exacerbated by network administrators who lock down hardware to the point that even teachers cannot install software needed for instruction. Computers and other technologies are placed in labs instead of every classroom, severely limiting access and use. And even though a growing number of students own multiple mobile technologies, they are rarely allowed to use these technologies in the classroom.

Yes, kids make many poor decisions; however, making mistakes is part of growing up. We may not be able to shield students from this fact of life, but we can teach ethical use of whatever technologies come our way, identify ways to provide environments where making mistakes is less risky, and help them learn from their mistakes.

ETHICAL USE OF TECHNOLOGY

Much of the instruction provided today that is related to digital citizenship focuses on Internet safety and *stranger danger*. Although students need this information to be well-rounded digital citizens, it's just a small part of the picture. Left to their devices, there are students who are engaging in one or more undesirable behaviors ranging from cyber-bullying of one another and adults, to plagiarism, to behaviors that can be harmful to them personally—both now and in the future. But fear tactics and threats simply drive these behaviors underground. We need to teach children and teens responsible, ethical behaviors in ways that provide positive models and allow students to make mistakes they can learn from. There are three aspects to this approach to teaching digital citizenship: (1) respect yourself, (2) respect others, and (3) respect outside limits (rules and laws).

Respect Yourself

Students who are willing to endanger themselves online are likely to be engaging in similar behaviors offline as well. Teaching self-respect is not a new concept. We encourage parents to help their children learn self-respect, and we use a variety of programs and modeling techniques to teach self-respect at school as well. What may be lacking is talking specifically about self-respect and online behavior.

The Myth of Online Privacy

A surprising number of students think that personal space online is private space. Students who have been disciplined for inappropriate personal behavior based on something they've posted on a social network such as MySpace or Facebook frequently express surprise that a school official "invaded their privacy" by reading the posting. Clearly, students still do not understand that online posts, whether text, photos, or videos, are not private. Even when students opt to use privacy settings on a social networking profile or similar site (and many do not bother), it is possible for others to access this information. A Google search using the keywords "hacker access private profiles" yields 305,000 hits, many of which contain all the information needed to hack a variety of "private" pages.

Students must be taught that when they choose to use a venue as accessible and public as the Internet to express their deepest thoughts and feelings, they are choosing to expose themselves to anyone who might choose to read what they've posted—including parents and school officials. They also need to be taught that the Internet sometimes creates a false sense of security. Users cannot see or hear their readers at the time they are posting, so they tend to ignore their presence, thinking that they are somehow cloaked in invisibility. Despite their feelings to the contrary, reading online posts is not snooping.

Anything students really want to keep private needs to stay offline. But for students to grasp this concept, parents and teachers need to provide opportunities for discussions and supervised use of social networks before students use publicly available sites. The news is rife with stories of students who think their online privacy was violated. Use these as the basis of class discussions. There are also ways to provide more protected environments for students to use classroom social networks. Elgg (http://elgg.org) and Drupal (http://drupal.org) are free, **open-source** software programs that can be downloaded and used to set up in-house social networks that, because they are self-contained, may be used by students of all ages. Web-based alternatives include Imbee (http://www.imbee.com/teacher) for children younger than 13 and Ning (http://www.ning.com) for

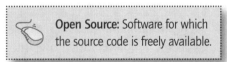

Open Source: Software for which the source code is freely available.

students older than 13. Ad-free Ning groups that will be used by students ages 13 to 17 are available to teachers on request.

Seeking Approval

In a contradictory vein, a few teens will also sometimes post photos or text that misrepresents something they've done or that they would normally not put online to impress other members of the social network and appear cool. So although they often think of postings as being private, there is also—at some level—recognition that other social networkers will be viewing what they post.

What they fail to understand is that these kinds of posts are the type that is most likely to attract unwanted attention along with the validation they are seeking. In addition, college admissions officers and prospective employers are Googling applicants' names to find and view online profiles. For example, more than 50% of human resources officers contacted in 2007 for a survey conducted by the Society for Human Resource Management indicated that they already Google job applicants prior to setting an interview or plan to begin doing so (Choi, 2009). When they find photos depicting rowdy or inappropriate behavior or read posts that describe the same, they don't take the time to analyze whether the posts are genuine. They simply move on to the next candidate. Again, many news stories are available on this topic for use as discussion starters, and teachers can use classroom networks to help students make wise decisions about what to post.

Internet Archiving

Students also are under the impression that they can delete an inappropriate posting and that will be the end of it. What they do not understand is that Web pages are archived and accessible in earlier versions, so nothing is ever actually deleted. The easiest way for teachers to demonstrate this is to plan an activity where students visit the WaybackMachine (http://www.archive.org/index.php), an Internet archive that can be accessed and searched by anyone.

As mentioned at the beginning of this section, students who do not respect themselves online are probably engaged in harmful behaviors offline as well. If, after discussions and activities related to online self-respect, an educator is still concerned about an individual student, it would be wise to implement school or district procedures for providing additional support and assistance through counseling or whatever other resources are available.

Respect Others

Being thoughtless, unintentionally or on purpose, is the basis of many of the problems that arise when using Web 2.0 tools. Researchers have a term for this behavior—*online disinhibition* (Suler, 2004). Basically, it means that people will say and do things online they would never dream of saying or doing in person. John Suler of Rider University identifies several factors that contribute to online disinhibition. These include online anonymity; invisibility, the ability to lurk and the ability to be physically invisible even when engaging with others online; asynchronous communication where the recipients' reactions are not immediate; the tendency to attribute qualities and characteristics to anonymous online contacts that may not be accurate or conversely to dehumanize the person on the other end of online communication; and the inclination to equalize everyone online, not knowing who individuals are or their real-world status.

These factors make it easy for adults to behave badly on the Internet, as in the case of Lori Drew, a parent in Missouri who was convicted of cyber-bullying one of her daughter's classmates (Risling, 2008). If adults engage in this kind of behavior, why do we expect that students will act differently? This does not excuse the lack of respect for others online, but it does underscore the critical importance of early and ongoing direct instruction about respecting others in online environments, particularly in relationship to respecting the privacy of others and cyber-bullying.

Respecting the Privacy of Others

It's probably safe to say that students who demonstrate self-respect on the Web are more likely to treat others with respect in person as well. Conversely, those who do not respect themselves will be more willing to disrespect others. A common gaffe committed by many students is posting information about others without their permission. This most often involves photos and video, but it can also include written material in the form of posts, text messages, IMs, and the like.

This behavior is usually thoughtless rather than mean-spirited, but it can have serious ramifications all the same. For example, Student A is concerned about her digital footprint—the amount and type of information available about her online. One precaution she takes is to keep her profile and comments on Facebook extremely neutral. Unfortunately, much of our digital footprint is beyond our control, as Student A learned recently.

Student B took a photo of Student A at an after-game party. In the photo, Student A was holding a red plastic cup, the type that beer drinkers favor. The cup actually contained soda. Without permission, Student B posted the photo, tagged it with Student A's name, the name of their school, and captioned it "The life of the party." In a few days, both students were called in to the assistant principal's office because she regularly checks Facebook for references to the school and found the photo. Parents were notified and disciplinary action was threatened. Although Student B was finally able to convince the assistant principal that the caption was meant to be sarcastic, the entirely unpleasant situation occurred all because Student B failed to respect Student A's right to privacy.

Teachers and parents usually teach children and teens about respecting the privacy of others, but do not always think to include online activities in these lessons. Educators cannot assume that students will transfer learning about face-to-face situations to online environments. Therefore, it's important to include specific references, examples, and activities related to the Internet. More information about the concept of digital footprint can be found on the Pew Internet & American Life Project Web site at the Growing Up site at http://www.growing-up-online.com/your_child_s_digital_footprint_68117.htm.

Legal Issues

As related to use of hardware, software, and the Internet in education settings, the legal landscape is less clearly defined than most adults would like. Two federal acts—the Children's Online Privacy Protection Act (COPPA) and the Children's Internet Protection Act (CIPA)—provide guidelines for protecting students' privacy and safety while online, and educational institutions that apply for certain federal funds must comply with these provisions. Copyright and fair use are also defined at the federal level.

Other issues, sexting or cyber-bullying, for example, are dealt with state by state, making it impossible to discuss these laws in any specific ways. However, those districts and schools receiving CIPA funds are required to have an Internet safety policy in place and to certify that students are receiving instruction in appropriate online behavior. This policy should provide guidance for administrators and educators in how to deal with misuse of technology and the Internet.

Effective Internet safety policies are revisited and updated annually. They are reviewed by attorneys to ensure that they can be enforced, are signed by students and their parents, and are kept on file. Teachers and administrators provide regular instruction in the provisions of the policy and model adherence to the rules themselves.

In cases where misuse is not specifically covered in the policy, it's important to think before acting. Teachers need to enlist the support of site administrators who, in turn, need to consult with district officials. This is not suggesting that you drag your feet in the hope that a problem will go away. It is a recommendation that you do your research and make a decision that is well reasoned, not caught up in the emotions of the moment.

Cyber-Bullying

Not all disregard of online privacy is benign. As explained in Chapters 2 and 8, cyber-bullying is the use of electronic media to threaten, harass, embarrass, or otherwise bully someone. Students who cyber-bully target both peers and adults and often have been victims of cyber-bullies themselves.

There have always been bullies, but what makes cyber-bullying such a serious problem is the fact that cyber-bullies can access their victims 24 hours a day. Cyber-bullies typically use cell phone text messages and cameras along with social networking sites, blogs, and Web pages to torment their victims and often provide online forums where readers are invited to add additional nasty remarks.

Parents of cyber-bullies and some educators tend to underestimate the impact of cyber-bullying. Parents excuse a child's behavior saying he or she was just blowing off steam or didn't mean anything by it. Educators often tell victims to toughen up or to ignore the bullying. But this is easier said than done. On the other hand, some adults overreact immediately, making the situation even worse.

Because of online disinhibition, it's easy to become a cyber-bully. The best way to deal with this problem is to bring it out in the open, but adults need to take a balanced approach. Many victims never report cyber-bullying, not because they fear their tormentor(s) but because they are afraid of the reactions of the adult they tell (CNET Yahoo! Tech, 2008).

Educators and parents need to be on the same page when it comes to the serious nature of cyber-bullying. This means that, besides educating students about this behavior, it is also necessary to educate parents. Teachers can access many online resources to find information, lesson plans, and other resources for working with parents and students. Here is a list of some of the better-known sites:

- Cyberbullying.us (http://www.cyberbullying.us/)
- Stop Cyberbullying (http://www.stopcyberbullying.org/index2.html)
- Center for Safe and Responsible Use of the Internet (http://www.cyber bully.org/)

Respect Outside Limits (Rules and Laws)

Few students are aware of the provisions of the school or district acceptable use policy or how policies against cheating and plagiarism can be applied to Internet use. In addition, few students are fully aware of laws that are applied to Internet use, including copyright and, a recent concern, distribution of child pornography. Because of the punitive nature of many of these policies and laws, students are facing extreme disciplinary actions and sometimes are being charged with felonies. Students need to face logical consequences for their actions, but in many cases, adults are taking what should be an opportunity to teach a life lesson and making it a scenario that will have a negative impact on the student for the rest of his or her life.

Acceptable Use Policies and Codes of Conduct

If your school is like most, a thick packet of papers is sent home the first day of the new school year. In that packet, there will be a code of conduct and an acceptable use policy. The hope is that parents will sit down with their children, review and discuss the materials, then sign the documents and send them back to school the next day. The reality is usually that parents, who have worked all day and are exhausted, will glance at the paperwork, sign it, and put it somewhere they hope the student will see it and pick it up on the way out the door the following morning.

Once the papers arrive back at school, they are collected and filed. There are some conscientious administrators and teachers who will do a quick review of the code of conduct and acceptable use policy shortly thereafter, but that's typically all the instruction students get until someone gets in trouble. At that point, the students may be genuinely confused by how much real trouble they are in, especially when the difficulty relates to misuse of technology.

A more effective approach is to take the time at the start of the year to educate parents about the contents of these documents—perhaps during back to school night—and to carefully review behavior expectations and the acceptable use policy with students. Then, review these documents at least two to three additional times during the school year. It's also important to ensure that students clearly understand the consequences of not following the policies.

To really make an impression on students, teachers and administrators need to model appropriate behaviors as well. If it's not okay for students to receive personal calls during class, it's probably not a good idea for teachers to answer their cell phones during class either. Or if students are not supposed to check their Facebook profile on school equipment, adults should probably not look in on an online auction or take care of other personal business on the Internet.

Cheating and Plagiarism

Technology-based cheating is a hot issue these days. Students take photos of tests and send them to friends and text one another during tests to share answers. Or kids go online and purchase prewritten term papers or copy and paste articles they turn in as their own.

Most classroom assessment is designed using a paradigm of education firmly rooted in the 19th and 20th centuries, when rote memorization and being able to feed back basic facts was enough education for most people. Today's students cannot memorize everything they will need to know throughout their lifetimes. They need to know where to go to find information, how to evaluate the accuracy of that information, and how to synthesize what they've learned to apply the knowledge to complete a task. They also need to learn how to work with others throughout this process.

If educators take the time to redesign assessments to reflect these new information literacy skills, they can eliminate most cheating on tests. This is because students would be encouraged to work together and use all the resources at their disposal to find workable solutions or correct answers to questions posed in the exam. Of course, this type of exam will be more difficult for students to complete in one class period and will be more difficult to grade, but the benefits would outweigh the extra work.

When students purchase term papers online, they know a rule is being broken. However, when students copy and paste text and images, they often do not know they are violating copyright laws. Educators need to teach students about copyright and fair use to ensure that they understand what they may do with information they find online. There are many resources teachers can use to educate students about copyright. They include the following:

- Copyright Kids (http://www.copyrightkids.org/)
- Williams College Libraries (http://library.williams.edu/copyright.php)
- Students as Creators: Exploring Copyright (http://www.readwritethink .org/lessons/lesson_view.asp?id=1085)

Teaching digital citizenship skills is an ongoing proposition. As new technologies with new features are introduced, students will come up with ways to use them that adults did not anticipate. Some of these uses will be creative and innovative while other uses will be harmful. The important thing is to remember that whatever kids come up with can be addressed and should not be used as an excuse to ban an otherwise useful technology.

DISCUSSION POINTS

1. Does your school or district have a policy about teaching Internet safety? If so, describe the curriculum and explain the requirements of the program. If not, explain how you deal with Internet safety issues.

2. Many prosecutors are charging students who participate in sexting with felonies. What do you think of this practice, and how would you handle the situation at your school or in your district?

3. Does your district or site have a copyright policy in place? How are teachers and students made aware of copyright law, and who monitors for adherence to these laws?

4. Describe the characteristics of a model digital citizen. How well do the adults and students at your workplace meet your definition?

REFERENCES

Web Sites

Center for Safe and Responsible Use of the Internet. (2009). http://www.cyber bully.org/.
Copyright Kids. (2009). http://www.copyrightkids.org/.
Cyberbullying.us. (2009). http://www.cyberbullying.us/.
Drupal. (2009). http://drupal.org/.
Elgg. (2009). http://elgg.org.
Growing Up Online. (2009). http://www.growing-up-online.com/your_child_s_ digital_footprint_68117.htm.
Pew Internet & American Life Project. (2009). http://www.pewinternet.org/.
Stop Cyberbullying. (2009). http://www.stopcyberbullying.org/index2.html.
Students as Creators: Exploring Copyright. (2009). http://www.readwrite think.org/lessons/lesson_view.asp?id=1085.
WaybackMachine. (2009). http://www.archive.org/index.php/.
Williams College Libraries. (2009). http://library.williams.edu/copyright.php.

Online Reports and Articles

Choi, C. (2009, February 1). Prying eyes: Play it safe with your online profile. *The Seattle Times*. Retrieved from http://seattletimes.nwsource.com/html/business technology/2008694402_onlineprofiles01.html.
CNET, Yahoo! Tech. (2008, October 4). *Kids keep parents in the dark about cyberbullying*. Retrieved from http://tech.yahoo.com/news/net/20081004/ tc_cnet/8301102331005844493.
Risling, G. (2008, November 26.) Jury convicts Missouri mom of misdemeanors in cyberbullying case. *Columbia Missourian*. Retrieved from http://www.columbia missourian.com/stories/2008/11/26/missouri-mom-convicted-lesser-charges-online-hoax/.
Suler, J. (2004). The online disinhibition effect. *Cyber Psychology and Behavior, 7*, 321–326. Retrieved from http://www-usr.rider.edu/~suler/psycyber/disin hibit.html.

Decision-Making 11 and Implementation Model

Who makes the decisions for your school or district when it comes to incorporating a new technology, software program, or Web site into instruction? If your situation is similar to that of a majority of U.S. educators, the decision about whether to adopt an emerging technology is often made by IT staff members who have little or no background in instruction, or the decision is made in reaction to an unanticipated consequence or problem that arises.

This approach to selection and implementation of 21st-century instructional tools and strategies is problematic on several levels. This chapter provides a brief discussion about who needs to be involved in making decisions about the use of emerging technologies and the critical importance of being proactive when planning and identifying steps that can be set in play by school leaders to either avoid or neutralize problems (unexpected and otherwise) that arise. Finally, this chapter includes a decision-making model that school and district leaders can use when considering use of one or more emerging technologies.

WHO'S CALLING THE SHOTS?

Becoming an IT professional requires a number of certifications, but a teaching credential isn't a license held by most of the IT staff who work in schools or districts. Although teaching experience is not a prerequisite for keeping the infrastructure up and running, it would benefit educators and IT staff greatly if the latter group had a deeper understanding of how technology is used for teaching and learning. Similarly, it would be helpful if educators had a better idea of the challenges IT staff face when it comes to keeping the network operational.

What are some of the IT challenges? Usage patterns for school networks are very different from business networks. For example, in most business settings a predictable number of employees use the network throughout the workday. But in schools, usage can fluctuate dramatically depending on the time of day and class schedules. It's common to see long lulls where office staff members are the primary users to huge spikes when large groups of students on multiple campuses hit the network simultaneously. It's difficult for IT staff to ensure that network performance will be optimal no matter what time it is or how many users are accessing the Web at once.

Besides traffic issues, IT staff need to guard against an array of viruses, worms, spam, and other attacks on the network that can originate online or through installation and uploading of infected files and software programs or unauthorized access using personal equipment. Finally, schools or districts accepting federal funds in certain categories are also required to institute stringent Internet filtering policies to protect students' online safety. It's no wonder that many IT departments decide to keep the network locked down as tightly as possible.

The problem with this approach to network security is that it interferes with instruction. Although teachers should plan ahead and know what sites and equipment they want to use before class begins, they also sometimes need to seize the teachable moment and deviate from their plan. In situations where filtering is very strict, this often means that perfectly safe instructional sites cannot be accessed on the spur of the moment because they've not been unblocked ahead of time.

Even when teachers follow established procedures for obtaining permission to use a new device, software program, or to get a site unblocked prior to class, follow-up is often dependent on the already heavily impacted schedules of IT staff who may, or may not, get to it before the lesson is taught. Or requests may be denied simply because an IT staff member does not personally understand why a particular technology tool should be used. This happens often when teachers want to try a new mobile device or Web 2.0 tool.

Problems of this type can be further exacerbated when the IT department falls under the domain of a district's business division because there may be limited or no communication with the divisions that deal with assessment, curriculum, and instruction. As a result, policies and decisions made tend to focus primarily on the health of the infrastructure rather than the needs of the teachers and students. As emerging technologies play an increasingly important role in establishing 21st-century learning environments, there is a growing need for greater cooperation and collaboration between IT departments and those divisions dealing with instructional issues. But this won't happen without making conscious decisions to change current procedures. All staff—certificated, noncertificated, and administrative—must be engaged in revising and implementing procedures that support decision making that keeps the focus on what's best for students.

THINKING AHEAD

Even when IT and instructional staff are working in concert, things do not always work as planned. Widespread use of technology as a tool to support teaching and learning is still in its infancy, and it's nearly impossible to predict all the unintended consequences—positive and negative—of introducing emerging technologies into schools. Most of the problems that arise can be addressed through professional development for educators, student instruction, and good home/school communication. But if educators have not anticipated what might happen, they will end up caught off guard and may not come up with the best solutions when under pressure.

Each previous chapter in this book includes a discussion of the common objections raised when educators consider using specific mobile technologies or Web 2.0 tools. Unfortunately, these objections are often used as deal breakers. Although it's important that these concerns be put on the table, the driving purpose should be to enable educators to have open discussions about potential unintended consequences. Once everyone's concerns are out in the open, it's possible to consider solutions or strategies for working around problems.

What are examples of unintended consequences that have already cropped up? Online testing makes it easy to score exams and get results almost immediately, so some states have adopted statewide online testing programs. Unfortunately, many districts do not have enough equipment to support one-to-one testing. As a result, the computers that are onsite have been placed in labs where they are in use the majority of the time for test taking, not instruction. Although the intent was not to further limit student access to technology, this has been the result.

Another example relates to one-to-one initiatives where students are each provided a laptop and access to a wireless network, but no resources are allocated to help teachers make changes in the design of classroom activities or instructional practices. Because some teachers continue to rely heavily on direct instruction, bored students tend to surf the Web (instead of writing paper notes to one another). In very short order, these teachers start insisting that students keep the laptops closed during class. Because of a lack of effective support, the initiative is written off as a waste of time and money.

The Children's Online Privacy Protection Act (COPPA) has also had unintended consequences. Written in 1998, the law includes a provision that bans children under the age of 13 from using Web sites that require personal information to sign up for an account (including e-mail addresses). The only exception to this rule is those Web sites where the company is willing to maintain extensive records to demonstrate that the information is secure and kept private. Many of the Web 2.0 sites that support collaboration require an e-mail address to access files stored online, but they do not have the resources to keep up with the federally required documentation. This means that in many instances, children under the age of 13 who would benefit from using a site are not allowed to do so. Once again, an unanticipated consequence gets in the way of student learning.

DECISION-MAKING MODEL

Few school districts have an established process for reviewing emerging technology tools for classroom use, or they rely on one that is outdated. The following model (pages 115–120) encourages educators to work collaboratively in grade level or departmental teams, as members of site or district technology committees, or as members of instruction review teams to carefully consider each emerging technology based on its merits and potential for classroom use. Teams may also invite students, parents, and other community members to take part in this process.

Each step in the decision-making model includes specific directions for use and forms to complete during information gathering and discussions prior to making decisions. Because this field is rapidly changing, the model design is open-ended to ensure applicability for some time.

Step 1

Clarifying the Issues		
Technology/tool under consideration:		
What are the reasons for using this technology/tool?	What are the concerns about using this technology/tool?	What are the questions we have about using this technology/tool?
How can we enhance or expand our ideas about using this technology/tool?		
How can we address our concerns about using this technology/tool?		

Step 2

Laying the Groundwork			
Technology/tool under consideration:			
What questions must be answered before we pursue use of this technology?	Where can we find the answers to our questions?	Who will research these questions?	When will they report back?

Step 3

Owning the Decision	
Technology/tool under consideration:	
Who is likely to support use of this technology?	How can we engage these people in the plan?
Who is likely to resist use of this technology?	How can we turn these people into supporters or deflect resistance?
What is our decision about the use of this technology to support learning and teaching?	

Step 4

Next Steps		
Technology/tool under consideration:		
Action Step	Who Is Responsible?	Due Date

Step 5

Individual Action Steps			
Technology/tool under consideration:			
Action step:			
How much time is required?	What human resources are needed?	What fiscal resources are needed?	What technical resources are needed?

Step 6

Evaluation			
Technology/tool under consideration:			
Action Step	Success Indicators	Data Source	Due Date

This is an exciting time to be an educator. The possibilities for reaching and engaging students are growing daily. As new tools for communication and collaboration continue to be developed and made readily available to people around the world, educators continually need to adapt their approach to instruction to ensure that classroom activities remain relevant. Fortunately, these changes are doable. All that's required is the will to move forward.

Glossary

Aggregator: An online service that allows users to subscribe to audio and video channels to access files to download for use on an MP3 player.

Avatar: When used in reference to virtual worlds, an avatar is a two- or three-dimensional graphic representation of a person or animal, which often can be personalized. Players interact with one another in the virtual world through their avatars.

Blog: Online writing tool that consists of dated entries posted in reverse chronological order so the most recent entry appears first.

Children's Online Privacy Protection Act of 1998: Also called COPPA, this act describes the kinds of information that may or may not be collected from children under the age of 13 when they are online. It also sets out guidelines that Web site operators must include in their privacy policies.

Complex Games: As defined by Marc Prensky, these games usually require at least 20 hours to complete but may take 100 or more hours. Complex games offer multiple levels of play, each of which provides multifaceted challenges, goals, or missions that must be completed to move to the next level. Players are required to learn multiple skills, and many complex games must be played by teams.

Cyber-Bullying: Use of electronic means to threaten, harass, humiliate, or embarrass the victim.

Digital Audio Player: Also called a DAP, this device is used to store, organize, and play audio files.

Digital Literacy: Ability to accurately locate, understand, analyze, and evaluate information using digital tools.

Flash Memory: A kind of memory chip that retains information even without a power source. For example, USB drives use flash technology as do digital cameras. Devices such as MP3 players and netbooks may use flash memory to store data.

Massive Multiplayer Online Game: An online game capable of supporting hundreds, even thousands, of players.

Media Player Program: Software that is preinstalled on computers that allows users to listen to or view audio and video files stored on the computer. Real Media Player and iTunes are examples.

Meme: A catch phrase or concept that spreads quickly from person to person via the Internet.

Microblogging: A form of blogging that limits message length—typically to 140 characters or less.

Minigames: As defined by Marc Prensky, these games can usually be played in an hour or less and typically focus on one narrow topic. Multiple play levels may be available, but they are just more-difficult iterations of the same basic concept. Most educational games, both online and offline, fall into this category.

Mini-Laptop: This term is sometimes used to refer to a netbook.

Mobile Internet Device: Often shortened to MID, this term is sometimes used to refer to a netbook.

MPMan: The first publicly available MP3 players, initially sold in Korea in 1998.

MP3 Player: A digital audio player (DAPs) that is used to store, organize, and play audio files. The name "MP3" comes from the most popular format for these audio files.

Netbook: Small-size, lightweight mobile computing device designed to easily access the Internet using built-in wireless capability. Most netbooks carry a low price tag.

Open Source: Software for which the source code is freely available.

Personal Digital Assistants: Also called PDAs, these handheld devices are used for a variety of purposes from managing calendars and contacts, to gaming, to basic word processing, and to using other work-related applications.

Podcasting: Creating audio content (think radio) that is uploaded to an Internet site. Podcasts can be set up so anyone can listen, or they can be password protected to limit access.

Portable Media Player: Also called a PMP, this device is used to store, organize, and play audio files and supports viewing images and/or playing video.

RSS Feed: *RSS* is an acronym for really simple syndication. An RSS feed helps readers subscribe to blogs and other Web sites that are updated regularly to keep track of these updates and have handy access in one place.

Role-Playing Games: Games of this type encourage players to assume different identities and try various behaviors to see how they work.

Sexting: The act of sending sexually explicit material, usually photographs, from one cell phone to another.

Smart Phone: Cell phone with features that enable it to manage and transmit data as well as voice calls.

Social Network Services: "Web-based services that allow individuals to (1) construct a public or semi-public profile within a bounded system, (2) articulate a list of other users with whom they share a connection, and (3) view and traverse their list of connections and those made by others within the system. The nature and nomenclature of these connections may vary from site to site" (boyd & Ellison, 2007, ¶ 4).

Sub-Notebook: This term is sometimes used to refer to a netbook.

21st-Century Skills: The content knowledge and applied skills that today's students need to master to thrive in a continually evolving workplace and society.

Ultralight PC: Often shortened to ULPC, this term is sometimes used to refer to a netbook.

Ultra Mobile PC: Often shortened to UMPC, this term is sometimes used to refer to a netbook.

Virtual World: A three-dimensional, graphic representation of a community that can be based entirely on fantasy or have roots in a real community.

Web 2.0: The second generation of the World Wide Web with a shift away from static Web pages and a move toward content that is dynamic and can be shared.

Web-Based Word Processors: Applications that allow users to create, edit, and store files online and then publish these files on the Internet, when appropriate.

Wiki: A Web site that allows visitors to add, remove, and edit content.

Web Sites by Topic

21st-Century Skills	
Web Site Title	**URL**
Core Knowledge Foundation	http://coreknowledge.org/CK/index.htm
International Society for Technology in Education (ISTE)	http://www.iste.org/
Partnership for 21st Century Skills	http://www.21stcenturyskills.org/
Cell Phones	
Web Site Title	**URL**
Cinch	http://cinch.blogtalkradio.com/
CTIA: The Wireless Association	http://www.ctia.org
Drop.io	http://drop.io/
FCC Kids Zone	http://www.fcc.gov/cgb/kidszone/
Flickr	http://flickr.com
MobiOde	http://www.mobiode.com/
Polleverywhere	http://www.polleverywhere.com/
Shutterfly	http://www.shutterfly.com/
MP3 Players	
Web Site Title	**URL**
Education Podcast Network	http://epnweb.org/
Grandview Library Blog	http://www.grandviewlibrary.org/
How Stuff Works	http://electronics.howstuffworks.com
iTunes	http://www.apple.com/itunes/
Juice	http://juicereceiver.sourceforge.net/

(Continued)

(Continued)

LearnOutLoud.com	http://www.learnoutloud.com/
PodcastDirectory.org.uk	http://www.podcastdirectory.org.uk/
Radio WillowWeb	http://www.mpsomaha.org/willow/radio/index.html
Speaking of History	http://speakingofhistory.blogspot.com/
Teachers Teaching Teachers	http://teachersteachingteachers.org/
Wikimedia Commons	http://commons.wikimedia.org/wiki/Main_Page

Netbooks	
Web Site Title	**URL**
Acer	http://www.acer.com
ASUS	http://asus.com/
Eee PC Pilot, TannerVision	http://tannervision.blogspot.com/search/label/EeePC%20pilot
HP	http://www.hp.com/
One Laptop per Child	http://laptop.org/

Social Networks	
Web Site Title	**URL**
Alexa	http://www.alexa.com/
Facebook	http://www.facebook.com/
MySpace	http://www.myspace.com/

Virtual Worlds	
Web Site Title	**URL**
Disney's Club Penguin	www.clubpenguin.com/
Habbo	www.habbo.com/
Jumpstart	http://www.jumpstart.com/
Mokitown	http://www.mokitown.com/
Poptropica	http:// www.poptropica.com/
SecretBuilders	http:// www.secretbuilders.com/
Skoolaborate Blog	http://www.skoolaborate.com/

Teen Second Life	http://teen.secondlife.com/
There.com	http:// www.there.com/
Virtual Worlds Management	http://www.virtualworldsmanagement.com
Webkinz	http:// www.webkinz.com
Whyville	http://www.whyville.net/

Creating Content—Writing	
Web Site Title	**URL**
Blogger	http://www.blogger.com/
Edublogs	http://edublogs.org/
Google Docs	http://docs.google.com/
Jaiku	http://www.jaiku.com/
Many Voices 2009	http://manyvoices.wikispaces.com/
PBWorks	http://pbworks.com/
Plurk	http://www.plurk.com/
Twitter	http://twitter.com/
Wetpaint	http://www.wetpaint.com/
Wikispaces	http://www.wikispaces.com/
WordPress	http://wordpress.com/
Writeboard	http://www.writeboard.com/
Zoho Writer	http://writer.zoho.com

Creating Content—Images and Video	
Web Site Title	**URL**
Slide	http://www.slide.com
Comiqs	http://comiqs.com/
COPPA-Children's Online Privacy Protection Act	http://www.coppa.org/
Glogster	http://edu.glogster.com/
Google Docs	http://docs.google.com
Stanford University—Copyright & Fair Use	http://fairuse.stanford.edu/

(Continued)

(Continued)

U.S. Copyright Office	http://www.copyright.gov/
Zoho Show	http://show.zoho.com/
Gaming	

Web Site Title	**URL**
Alice	http://www.alice.org/
CivWorld	http://civworld.gameslearningsociety.org/
Classroom 2.0	http:// www.classroom20.com/
The Education Arcade	http://www.educationarcade.org/
futurelab—Teaching with Games	http://www.futurelab.org.uk/projects/teaching-with-games/
Game Maker: YoYo Games	http://www.yoyogames.com/make
GamesParentsTeachers.com	http://www.gamesparentsteachers.com/
History of Toys Timeline—History.com	http://www.history.com/content/toys/timeline
North American Simulation and Gaming Association (NASAGA)	http://www.nasaga.org/
Simple—Free Programming Language for Kids	http://www.simplecodeworks.com/website.html
Digital Citizenship	

Web Site Title	**URL**
Center for Safe and Responsible Use of the Internet	http://www.cyberbully.org/
Copyright Kids	http://www.copyrightkids.org/
Cyberbullying.us	http://www.cyberbullying.us/
Drupal	http://drupal.org/
Elgg	http://elgg.org
Growing Up Online	http://www.growing-up online.com/your_child_s_digital_footprint_68117.htm
Pew Internet & American Life Project	http://www.pewinternet.org/

Stop Cyberbullying	http://www.stopcyberbullying.org/index2.html
Students as Creators: Exploring Copyright	http://www.readwritethink.org/lessons/lesson_view.asp?id=1085
WaybackMachine	http://www.archive.org/index.php/
Williams College Libraries	http://library.williams.edu/copyright.php

Index

CORWIN
A SAGE Company

The Corwin logo—a raven striding across an open book—represents the union of courage and learning. Corwin is committed to improving education for all learners by publishing books and other professional development resources for those serving the field of PreK–12 education. By providing practical, hands-on materials, Corwin continues to carry out the promise of its motto: **"Helping Educators Do Their Work Better."**